a b c d e f g h i j k l m n o p q r s t u v w x y z

The Usborne
first
dictionary

with over 700 internet links

Rachel Wardley and Jane Bingham

Designed by Susie McCaffrey

Assistant designer: Sue Grobecker

Illustrated by Teri Gower
and Stuart Trotter

Photography by Mark Mason Studio

Advisors: John McIlwain, Rita D'Apice Gould and Porter Tierney

Finding a word

The words in a dictionary are arranged in alphabetical order from A to Z . This helps you to find them easily.

1 To find a word, such as "feeling", think of its first letter, "f".

2 Now look at the alphabet at the bottom of each page. When you see the letter "f" in a triangle, you have found the pages of "f" words.

3 Next, think of the second letter of your word. Look at the top of the page for words that begin "fe".

4 Then look down the "fe" words until you find your word.

Your word may not be in this dictionary, or you may have spelt it wrongly. Spelling panels, such as this one, will help you spell difficult words.

Some words that begin with an "f" sound, like **phone** and **photograph**, are spelt "ph".

Looking at a word

This dictionary tells you lots of things about words and how to use them.

You can check how to spell a word.

You can see other ways of using the word.

You can find out what the word means.

stretch

stretches stretching stretched

1 If you **stretch** something, you make it longer or bigger. *Simon stretched the rubber band until it snapped.*

2 When you **stretch**, you push your arms up or out as far as they will go. *Miriam stretched up high.*

You can see if a word has more than one meaning.

You can see how the word is used.

More help with words

Here are some ways that this dictionary helps you with writing, saying and understanding words.

It gives you ideas for other words to use in your writing.

Some other words for big are **enormous, gigantic, huge, massive** and **vast**.

It gives you the opposite of some words.

expensive
Something that is **expensive** costs a lot of money.
■ *opposite* **cheap**

It shows you how to say difficult words.

choir
choirs
A **choir** is a group of people who sing together.
▲ *say kwire*

It tells you where to find a picture of your word.

fly
flies
A **fly** is an insect with very thin, clear wings.
● *See* **insects** *on page 57.*

Alphabetical order

It's much easier to use a dictionary if you know how to put words into alphabetical order. See if you can do the Alphabetical animals quiz at the bottom of this page. Remember, to put words into alphabetical order, you compare their first letters, then their second letters, then their third, and so on.

For example, you put the words bed, ant, bedtime, bead, bedroom and bad into alphabetical order like this:

ant
bad   **a** *comes before* **b**
bead   **ba** *comes before* **be**
bed   **bea** *comes before* **bed**
bedroom   **bed** *comes before* **bedr**
bedtime   **bedr** *comes before* **bedt**

Alphabetical animals quiz

Can you put the names of these animals into alphabetical order? The answers are on page 144.

chimpanzee

bear

crocodile

chicken

crab

caterpillar

beaver

You could write your own list of words and put them in order.

Internet links

Some of the words in this dictionary have a symbol next to them, like this:

flower

This means there is a Web site where you can find out more about that subject or do an activity. For a link to this Web site, and to all the other Web sites recommended in this book, go to **www.usborne-quicklinks.com** and enter the keywords "first dictionary". On the Usborne Quicklinks Web site you will also find downloadable picture puzzles that you can print out to practise your spelling and punctuation.

Internet safety

Before you use the Internet, ask an adult to read through these safety guidelines with you.

• Always ask an adult's permission before you connect to the Internet.

• When you are on the Internet, never give out any personal information, such as your full name, address or telephone number.

• If a Web site asks you to log in or register by typing in your name or e-mail address, ask permission of an adult first.

Note to parents

We recommend that children are supervised while on the Internet, that they do not use Internet Chat Rooms, and that you use Internet filtering software to block unsuitable material. Please ensure that your children read and follow the safety guidelines printed above. Usborne Publishing is not responsible for the content of any Web site other than its own.

Which meaning?

Which is the correct meaning for each of these words? Look up the words in your dictionary to see if you were right.

dessert
- A dessert is a large piece of dry land.
- A dessert is someone who feels lonely.
- A dessert is a sweet food.

mysterious
- Something that is mysterious cannot be found.
- If it is mysterious, the weather is very bad.
- If something is mysterious, it is hard to explain or understand.

infectious
- Food that is infectious does not taste very nice.
- If a disease is infectious, you can catch it from another person.
- If something is infectious, it is very important.

nephew
- Someone's nephew is their sister's or brother's son.
- Someone's nephew is their mother's brother.
- Someone's nephew is their sister's or brother's daughter.

Which word?

Your dictionary will help you to answer these questions. Check your answers in the dictionary or on page 144.

1 What is a small, furry animal and something that moves things on a computer screen? *Look on page 73.*

2 What creature has fins, scales and a tail? *Find out in the letter "f".*

3 What is the opposite of deep? *See page 32.*

4 What other words can you use instead of big? *See page 15.*

5 What is a hard rock and a small glass ball? *Think of a word beginning with "m".*

6 How many shapes can you think of? *Look at page 106.*

7 What has handlebars, a headlight and an engine? *Look at the words beginning with "m".*

8 Bongos and maracas are both kinds of what? *See page 75.*

9 What other words can you use instead of bad? *See page 12.*

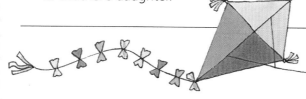

What am I?

Words that rhyme end with the same sound, so sad rhymes with bad and dish rhymes with fish. To find the answers to these clues, think of a word that rhymes with the one that you are given. The answers are on page 144.

I fly in the sky and I rhyme with fight.

You stand on me and I rhyme with jug.

I'm hard to see through and I rhyme with dog.

You ride me and I rhyme with like.

You read me and I rhyme with look.

USING WORDS

This dictionary shows you lots of ways of using words. Here is a list of different kinds of writing and the pages where you can find them.

Dear Simon
You wouldn't believe how hot it is here! The sea is amazingly clear and blue and we've been swimming every day. I've collected lots of shells and seen some really strange creatures in the rock pools. See you soon.
Lucy

Simon Small
12 Hilltop Road
CASTLETOWN
Wessex
UK

Adding words

Can you fill in the missing words in this story? Choose from the words in the box. You can read the completed story on page 144.

pebbles   top   heavy
reach   bottom   jug   drink
stream   thirsty   dropped
beak   work   idea

One hot day, a _____ crow called Caspar was searching for something to drink. The _____ had dried up and there was no water anywhere.

In the distance, Caspar saw a ___ on a table outside a cottage. He flew over to have a look. "Ah, there's water at the _____," he said. But he could not _____ it. Caspar felt more and more thirsty. He tried to push over the jug, but it was so _____ that he could not move it.

Then he had an _____. He flew off to a pile of pebbles and picked one up in his ____. Caspar flew back, _____ a pebble into the jug and then went off to find another. He dropped so many _____ into the jug that they pushed the water up to the ___. At last, he could have a long, cool ____. "All my hard ____ was worth it in the end," thought clever Caspar.

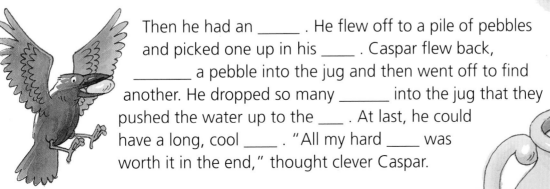

Aa

able
If you are **able** to do something, you know how to do it. *Zak is able to ride a bicycle.*

about
1 **About** means to do with something. *This book is about elephants.*
2 **About** also means near to something. *The party ends at about six o'clock.*

above
If something is **above** another thing, it is over it. *The balloons floated above the fair.*
■ *opposite* **below**

abroad
When you go **abroad**, you go to another country.

absent
If someone is **absent**, they are not here. *Joanna was absent from school today.*

accident
accidents
1 If there is an **accident**, something bad happens that you do not expect. *Rosa had an accident and broke her leg.*
2 If something happens by **accident**, nobody has planned or expected it. *I met my friend Peter by accident.*

ache
aches aching ached
If part of your body **aches**, it hurts. *Skating makes my legs ache.*
▲ *rhymes with cake*

across
If you walk **across** the road, you go from one side to the other.

act
acts acting acted
1 When you **act**, you do something. *Ranjit acted quickly to put out the fire.*
2 If you **act** in a play, you pretend to be one of the people in it.

activity
activities
An **activity** is something that you do. *Horse riding is my favourite activity.*

add
adds adding added
1 If you **add** something to another thing, you put it with that thing. *Add butter to the flour.*
2 When you **add** numbers, you put them together. *Jane added five and seven.*

5+7=12

address
addresses
Your **address** is the name of the place where you live.

Miss Miranda Moss
12 Princes Street
KINGSTOWN
Queenshire
K13 2BE

admire
admires admiring admired
If you **admire** someone or something, you think that they are very nice or very good. *Joe admired Rachel's painting.*

adopt
adopts adopting adopted
When people **adopt** a child, the child comes to live with them and becomes part of their family.

adult
adults
An **adult** is a grown-up person.

adventure
adventures
An **adventure** is something exciting that people do. Some adventures can be dangerous. *Exploring the castle was a great adventure.*

aeroplane
aeroplanes
An **aeroplane** is a large machine that flies through the air. Aeroplanes have wings and engines. They carry people or things from one place to another.

afford
affords affording afforded
If you can **afford** something, you have enough money to buy it.

afraid
If you are **afraid**, you think something bad will happen. *Jessie is afraid that Mike will fall out of the tree.*

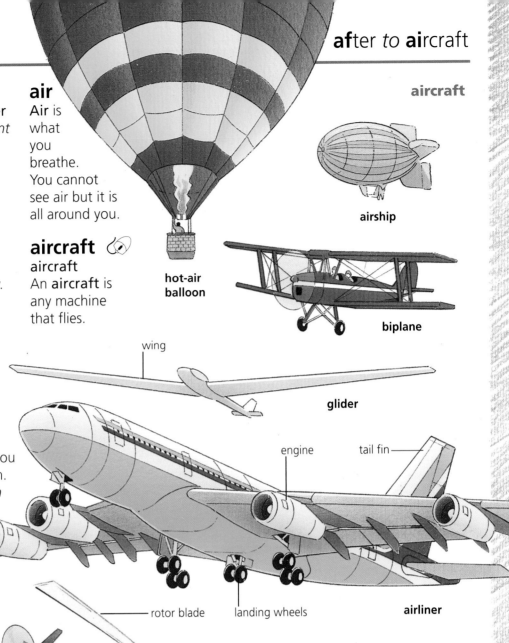

aircraft

after

1 When one thing happens **after** another, it happens later. *We went for a walk* **after** *lunch.*

■ *opposite* **before**

2 **After** also means following something. *William ran* **after** *the ball.*

afternoon

afternoons

The **afternoon** is part of the day. It starts at 12 o'clock and ends about 6 o'clock.

again

If you do something **again**, you do it one more time. *Beth is singing that song* **again***.*

against

1 If you are **against** someone, you are on a different side from them. *The teams will play* **against** *each other tomorrow.*

2 If something is **against** another thing, it is next to it and touching it. *Billy leant his bicycle* **against** *the wall.*

age

ages

Your **age** is how old you are.

ago

Ago means before now. *We started school two weeks* **ago***.*

agree

agrees agreeing agreed

If you **agree** with someone, you both think the same about something. *Garth and I* **agreed** *that the film was dreadful.*

ahead

If you are **ahead** of someone, you are in front of them. *Kim ran on* **ahead** *of the others. Susie is* **ahead** *of Sasha in maths.*

air

Air is what you breathe. You cannot see air but it is all around you.

aircraft

aircraft

An **aircraft** is any machine that flies.

hot-air balloon

airship

biplane

wing

glider

engine

tail fin

rotor blade

landing wheels

airliner

helicopter

cockpit

jet

propeller

float

seaplane

airport

airports

An **airport** is a place where aircraft take off and land.

alarm

alarms

An **alarm** is something that makes a loud noise. Alarms wake you up or warn you about something. *A fire alarm.*

album

albums

An **album** is a book with blank pages. You can stick photographs, stamps or pictures in an album.

alien

aliens

In stories, an **alien** is someone or something that comes from another planet. *Four aliens climbed out of the spacecraft.*

alike

If people are **alike**, they look the same. *The twins are alike.*

alive

If a person, an animal or a plant is **alive**, they are living.

■ *opposite* **dead**

all

All means everything, everyone, or the whole thing. *All the children were excited. Karen ate all the chocolate.*

alligator

alligators

An **alligator** is a reptile that looks like a crocodile, but has a flatter head and a shorter nose.

allow

allows allowing allowed

If someone **allows** you to do something, they let you do it. *Mum allowed us to stay up late.*

all right

Something that is **all right** is good enough. *Does this hat look all right?*

almost

Almost means close to. *It's almost bedtime.*

alone

When you are **alone**, you are not with anyone else.

along

1 If you walk **along** a street, you walk from one end of it to the other.
2 If you bring something **along**, you bring it with you. *Lee always brings his dog along when we go out together.*

aloud

When you read **aloud**, you read so that other people can hear you. *Nicole is reading her poem aloud.*

alphabet

alphabets

An **alphabet** is a set of all the letters that people use to write words. The letters in an alphabet are in a special order.

already

If something has happened **already**, it has happened before now. *I've seen this film already.*

also

You use the word **also** to mean something extra. *Hannah ate an apple. She also ate my banana.*

always

If you **always** do something, you do it all the time or every time. *I always read before I go to sleep.*
■ *opposite* **never**

amazing

Something that is **amazing** is very surprising. *Dan showed us an amazing trick.*

ambulance

ambulances

An **ambulance** is a special van that takes sick people to hospital.

amount

amounts

An **amount** is how much there is of something. *Sarah ate a tiny amount of ice cream. My brothers make a large amount of noise.*

anchor

anchors

An **anchor** is a heavy, metal hook on a long chain that is fixed to a ship. When the anchor is thrown off a ship, it sinks to the bottom of the sea and stops the ship from moving.

angry
angrier angriest
If you are **angry**, you feel upset and you often want to shout or fight with someone. *Kim was **angry** when she saw her broken glasses.*

animal
animals
An **animal** is anything that moves and breathes. Horses, lizards, fish, birds and insects are all animals. Plants are not animals.

ankle
ankles
Your **ankle** is the joint between your leg and your foot.

annoy
annoys annoying annoyed
If someone or something **annoys** you, they make you feel angry. *Ed **annoyed** his brother by singing.*

another
You use the word **another** to mean one more. *Please may I have **another** banana?*

answer
answers
An **answer** is what you say after someone has asked you a question. *Hari gave the right **answer** to the question.*

ant
ants
An **ant** is an insect. Ants live in large groups in the ground or in trees. *Some **ants** bite leaves from trees and carry them back to their nest.*

any
1 You use the word **any** to show that it does not matter which one. *Take **any** book you like.*
2 **Any** also means some. *Are there **any** biscuits left?*

apart
1 **Apart** means away from something else. *Stand with your feet **apart**.*
2 If you take something **apart**, you take it to pieces. *Ben is taking his bicycle **apart** to see how it works.*

ape
apes
An **ape** is a large animal with long arms and no tail. Apes can walk and stand like human beings.

apologize
apologizes apologizing apologized
When you **apologize**, you say sorry for something that you have done or said. *Mark **apologized** for breaking the chair.*

appear
appears appearing appeared
When something **appears**, it can be seen. *Two birds **appeared** from inside the hat.*
■ opposite **disappear**

apple
apples
An **apple** is a rounded fruit with a green, red or yellow skin.

apron
aprons
You wear an **apron** to keep your clothes clean when you are cooking or painting.

aquarium
aquariums
An **aquarium** is a glass tank filled with water. You keep fish and other creatures in an aquarium.

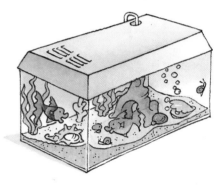

area
areas
An **area** is a place or a space. *A science **area**. A large **area** of grass.*

aren't
Aren't is a short way of saying **are not**. *These strawberries **aren't** ripe yet.*

 A B C D E F G H I J K L M N O P Q R S T U V W X Y Z

argue
argues arguing argued
People **argue** because they do not agree about something. When they argue, they say what they think and often get angry. *We argued about which team was the best.*

argument
arguments
You have an **argument** when you do not agree with someone. When people have an argument they say what they think and often get angry.

arm
arms
Your **arm** is the part of your body between your shoulder and your hand.

armchair
armchairs
An **armchair** is a comfortable chair with parts on either side for you to rest your arms on.

armour
Armour is a set of clothes made of metal. Soldiers wore armour long ago to protect themselves when they were fighting.

army
armies
An **army** is a large group of people who fight in a war.

around
1 Around means in a circle. *Mo tied a ribbon **around** her waist.*
2 Around also means in every part. *I looked **around** the house.*
3 Around can also mean near to something. *Kit lives **around** here.*

arrange
arranges
arranging
arranged
1 If you arrange things, you put them together so that they look tidy or pretty.
*Rana is **arranging** some flowers.*
2 When you **arrange** something, you plan how it will be done. *Mum is **arranging** a party for next weekend.*

arrive
arrives arriving arrived
When something or someone **arrives**, they get to where they are going. *The parcel **arrived** at Carla's house. We **arrived** at the park.*

arrow
arrows
1 An **arrow** is a thin stick with a point at one end and feathers at the other end. You shoot arrows from a bow.
2 An **arrow** is also a sign that shows you which way to go. *Follow the **arrows** to get to the sports hall.*

art
Art is something beautiful that has been made by someone. Paintings and drawings are types of art.

ask
asks asking asked
1 If you **ask** a question, you say that you want to know something. *Jim **asked** me how old I was.*
2 If you **ask** for something, you say that you want it. *Lorna **asked** for an apple.*

asleep
When you are **asleep**, your eyes are closed and your whole body is resting.
*Pickle is **asleep** on a cushion.*

assembly
assemblies
An **assembly** is a large group of people who are meeting together. *School **assembly**.*

astonish
astonishes astonishing astonished
If you **astonish** someone, you make them feel very surprised.

astronaut
astronauts
An **astronaut** is someone who goes into space. Astronauts travel in spacecraft.

astronaut

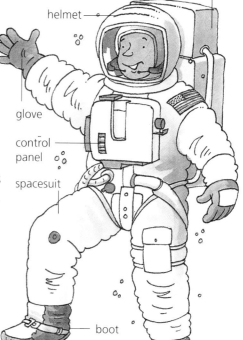

air tank

helmet

glove

control panel

spacesuit

boot

ate

Ate comes from the word **eat**.
Usually we eat at home. Yesterday we ate at a restaurant.

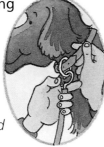

atlas

atlases
An **atlas** is a book of maps.

attach

attaches attaching attached
When you **attach** one thing to another, you join them together. *Tim attached the lead to Fido's collar.*

attack

attacks attacking attacked
If someone **attacks** another person, they try to hurt them.

attention

When you pay **attention**, you watch and listen carefully. *Pay attention to what I'm saying!*

attic

attics
An **attic** is a room at the top of a house, just under the roof.

attic

attract

attracts attracting attracted
When a magnet **attracts** an object, it makes it come nearer.

audience

audiences
An **audience** is a group of people who watch or listen to something, such as a play or a piece of music.

aunt

aunts
Your **aunt** is the sister of your mum or your dad. Your uncle's wife is also your aunt. Another word for aunt is auntie.

autumn

Autumn is one of the four seasons of the year. It comes between summer and winter. In the autumn, the weather begins to get cold and leaves fall from the trees.
▲ *say or-tum*

awake

Awake means not asleep. *Owls stay awake at night and sleep in the day.*

awful

Something that is **awful** is very bad. *An awful meal.*

awkward

1 Something that is **awkward** is difficult to use. *My shoelaces are awkward to tie because they are too short.*
2 Someone who moves in an **awkward** way is clumsy.
3 Someone who behaves in an **awkward** way is very hard to please.

axe

axes
An **axe** is a tool with a long handle and a large, metal blade. People use axes to chop wood.

Bb

baby

babies
A **baby** is a very young child.

baby-sitter

baby-sitters
A **baby-sitter** is someone who looks after children when their parents are out.

back

backs
1 The **back** of something is the part farthest from the front. *We sat at the back of the cinema.*
■ *opposite* front
2 Your **back** is the part of your body between your neck and your bottom.

backwards

1 If a word is spelt **backwards**, it is spelt the wrong way round. "Step" spelt backwards is "pets".
2 If you move **backwards**, you move the way that your back faces. *Jake is walking backwards through the snow.*
■ *opposite* forwards

back yard

back yards
A **back yard** is an area at the back of a house where you can play or grow plants.

bad
worse worst
1 Someone who is **bad** does things that they should not do.
■ *opposite* good
2 Something that is **bad** is not good. *A bad film.*
■ *opposite* good

> **Some other words for**
> bad are **awful**, **terrible** and **dreadful**.

badge
badges
A **badge** is a small picture that you wear on your clothes.

badger
badgers
A **badger** is a black and white animal that lives underground.

bag
bags
You use a **bag** to hold or carry things. *A shopping bag.*

bake
bakes baking baked
When you **bake** food, you cook it in an oven.

balance
balances balancing balanced
If you **balance** something, you keep it steady so that it does not fall. *Mum balanced a ball on her nose.*

bald
balder baldest
A man who is **bald** has no hair on the top of his head.

ball
balls
A **ball** is a round object that you throw and catch.

ballet
Ballet is a kind of dance with special steps, that you do to music. Ballet often tells a story.
▲ *say bal-ay*

balloon
balloons
A **balloon** is a thin, rubber bag. When you blow into a balloon, it gets bigger.

banana
bananas
A **banana** is a long, curved fruit with a thick, yellow skin.

band
bands
1 A **band** is a group of people who play music together.
2 A **band** is also a strip that you put around something. *Alice is wearing a hair band.*

bandage
bandages
A **bandage** is a long strip of cloth. You wrap a bandage round a part of your body that has been hurt.

bang
bangs banging banged
If something **bangs**, it makes a sudden, loud noise. *The door banged in the wind.*

bank
banks
1 A **bank** is a safe place where people can keep their money. Banks sometimes lend money to people.
2 A **bank** is also the ground beside a river or a stream. *The goose stood on the bank.*

bar
bars
A **bar** is a long, thin piece of wood or metal.

barbecue
barbecues
A **barbecue** is a meal that is cooked outside on a fire.

bare
barer barest
1 If you are **bare**, you are not wearing any clothes.
2 If a cupboard is **bare**, it has nothing in it.

bark
Bark is the hard skin that covers a tree's trunk and branches.

bark
barks
barking
barked
When a dog **barks**, it makes a loud noise in its throat.

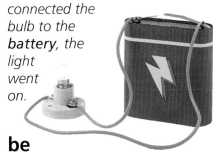

barn
barns
A **barn** is a large farm building. Straw, animals and machines are kept in barns.

barrel
barrels
A **barrel** is used to hold things. A barrel has curved sides and a flat top and bottom.

basket
baskets
You use a **basket** to carry things. Baskets can be made from strips of wood, wire or string.

bat
bats
1 A **bat** is a small, furry animal with wings. Bats sleep during the day and hunt for food at night.
2 A **bat** is also a kind of stick that you use to hit a ball.

bath
baths
A **bath** is a large container. You fill it with water and sit in it to wash.

battery
batteries
A **battery** is a tube or a box that makes electricity. You put batteries into torches, toys and radios to make them work. *When we connected the bulb to the battery, the light went on.*

be
is being was been
1 **Be** means to live or to take up space. *I want to **be** by the sea.*
2 The word **be** also shows what something is like. *I used to **be** shy.*

beach
beaches
A **beach** is a strip of sand or stones by the edge of the sea.

bead
beads
A **bead** is a small object with a hole through its middle. You can make necklaces with beads.

beak
beaks
A **beak** is the hard outside part of a bird's mouth.

bean
beans
A **bean** is a small vegetable. Beans often grow in pods.

bear
bears
A **bear** is a large, wild animal with thick fur. *Some **bears** catch fish to eat.*

beard
beards
A **beard** is the hair that grows on a man's chin and cheeks.

beat
beats beating
beat beaten
1 If you **beat** someone in a race or a competition, you do better than they do.
2 If you **beat** something, you keep hitting it. *Stuart **beat** his drum.*

beautiful
If something is **beautiful**, it is lovely to look at or listen to.

beaver
beavers
A **beaver** is an animal that lives in or near a river. It has very sharp teeth and a large, flat tail.

became
Became comes from the word **become**. *I hope the weather will become sunnier. Yesterday, it **became** sunny in the afternoon.*

 A B C D E F G H I J K L M N O P Q R S T U V W X Y Z

because

You use the word **because** to explain why something happens. *I was scared because it was dark.*

become

becomes becoming became become

If one thing **becomes** something else, it changes into it. *Some caterpillars become butterflies.*

bed

beds

A **bed** is something that you lie on when you sleep or rest.

bedroom

bedrooms

Your **bedroom** is the room where you sleep.

bedtime

bedtimes

Your **bedtime** is the time when you go to bed.

bee

bees

A **bee** is an insect with black and yellow stripes on its body. Some bees make honey.
● *See insects on page 57.*

beef

Beef is meat that comes from a cow.

beetle

beetles

A **beetle** is an insect with four wings. It has two soft wings that it uses for flying and two hard wings that protect its body.
● *See insects on page 57.*

before

If something happens **before** something else, it happens first.
■ *opposite* after

begin

begins beginning began begun

When you **begin** to do something, you start to do it. *Jo began to cry.*

behave

behaves behaving behaved
1 The way you **behave** is the way that you do things. *Annie is behaving very strangely today.*
2 If you **behave** yourself, you are good.

behind

If you are **behind** something, you are at the back of it. *Ramel hid behind the shed.*

believe

believes believing believed

If you **believe** something, you think that it is true. *Patrick always believes Buster's stories.*

bell

bells

A **bell** is a metal object shaped like a cup. Bells make a ringing noise when you hit them or shake them.

belong

belongs belonging belonged
1 If something **belongs** to you, it is yours. *This hat belongs to me.*
2 If you **belong** to a club, you are a member of it.
3 If something **belongs** in a place, that is where it should be. *The spade belongs in the shed.*

below

If something is **below** another thing, it is under it. *Katy sank below the surface of the water.*
■ *opposite* above

belt

belts

A **belt** is a thin band of leather, cloth or plastic that you wear around your waist. *Henry's belt stops his trousers falling down.*

bench

benches

A **bench** is a long, hard seat.

bend

bends bending bent

If something **bends**, it changes its shape so that it is not straight. *These straws bend in the middle.*

beneath

If something is **beneath** another thing, it is below it. *Spot is hiding beneath the table.*

bent

Bent comes from the word **bend**. *Grandma could not bend low enough to pick up her letters, so Honey bent down to get them.*

berry

berries

A **berry** is a small, soft fruit. Some berries are poisonous.

beside

If you are **beside** someone or something, you are next to them. *I sit beside Sam at school.*

best

Something that is the **best** is better than all the others. *Jan won a prize for doing the best painting.*
■ *opposite* worst

a b c d e f g h i j k l m n o p q r s t u v w x y z

better
1 You use the word **better** to mean very good compared with something else. *My bike is better than yours.*
2 If you feel **better**, you do not feel ill any more.

between
If you are **between** two things, you are in the middle of them.

beware
The word **beware** tells you to be careful because something is dangerous. *Beware of the bull.*

bicycle
bicycles
A **bicycle** is a vehicle with two wheels. You push the pedals to turn the wheels.

bicycle

saddle
handlebars
tyre
pedal
chain

big
bigger biggest
A **big** person or thing is large.
■ *opposite* small

Some other words for
big are **enormous**, **gigantic**, **huge**, **massive** and **vast**.

bike
bikes
Bike is short for **bicycle**.

bin
bins
You put rubbish in a **bin**.

bird
birds
A **bird** is an animal with two wings. Birds have beaks and are covered with feathers. Most birds can fly.

bird
throat
beak
wing
breast
claw
tail

birthday
birthdays
Your **birthday** is the date that you were born. People give you gifts every year on your birthday.

biscuit
biscuits
A **biscuit** is a small snack. Biscuits are baked in the oven until they are hard.

bite
bites biting bit bitten
When you **bite** something, you cut into it with your teeth. *Tamsin bit into a pear.*

bitter
If something tastes **bitter**, it has a sharp, sour taste. Orange peel tastes bitter.

black
Black is a colour. The letters on this page are black.

blackboard
blackboards
A **blackboard** is a black surface that you can write on with chalk.

blade
blades
A **blade** is the flat, sharp part of a knife that is used for cutting. Scissors have two blades.

blame
blames blaming blamed
If you **blame** someone, you think that they have made something bad happen. *Alexander blamed his brother for breaking his model aeroplane.*

blank
A **blank** piece of paper has nothing on it.

blanket
blankets
A **blanket** is a thick cover. You can put blankets on your bed to keep you warm.

bleed
bleeds bleeding bled
If you **bleed**, blood comes out of your body. *Jasper's nose bled when he bumped into the door.*

blew
Blew comes from the word **blow**. *Kim can blow very hard. She blew out all the candles on her cake.*

blind
Blind people cannot see.

blink
blinks blinking blinked
When you **blink**, you close and then open your eyes very quickly.

block
blocks
A **block** is a thick piece of something, such as wood or stone. Blocks usually have straight sides. *Building blocks.*

block
blocks blocking blocked
If something **blocks** the way, nothing can get past. *A fallen tree has blocked the road.*

blood
Blood is the red liquid inside your body. Your heart pushes blood round your body.

blouse
blouses
A **blouse** is a piece of clothing. Women and girls wear blouses on the top part of their bodies.

blow
blows blowing blew blown
1 When you **blow**, you push air out of your mouth. *Amy blew hard to put out all the candles.*
2 When the wind **blows**, it moves the air. *The wind has blown away dad's newspaper.*

blue
Blue is a colour. The sky on a sunny day is blue.

blunt
blunter bluntest
Something that is **blunt** is not sharp. *A blunt knife.*

board
boards
A **board** is a flat piece of wood or card. *A chess board.*

boast
boasts boasting boasted
Someone who **boasts** enjoys telling other people about what they have done or about the things that they own. *Annie is boasting about her new bicycle.*

boat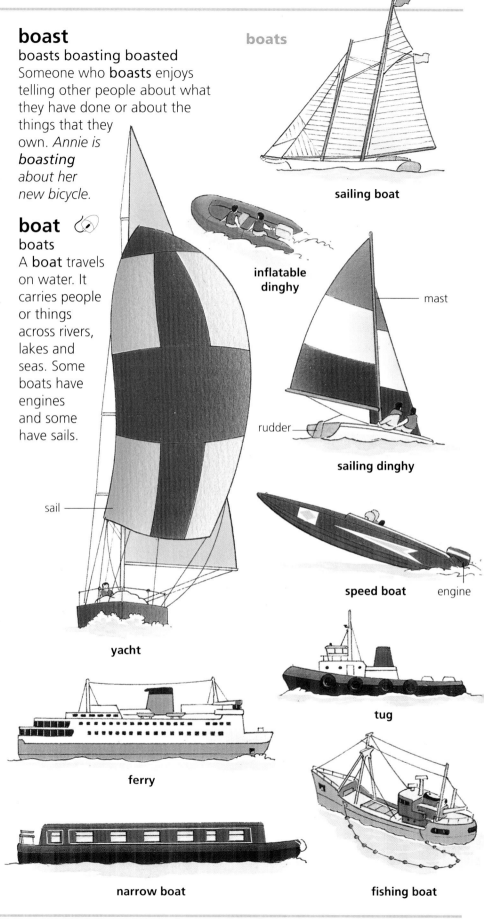
boats
A **boat** travels on water. It carries people or things across rivers, lakes and seas. Some boats have engines and some have sails.

boats

sailing boat

inflatable dinghy

mast

rudder

sailing dinghy

sail

speed boat   engine

yacht

tug

ferry

narrow boat

fishing boat

body
bodies

The **body** of a person or an animal is every part of them. Your legs, shoulders and head are all parts of your body.

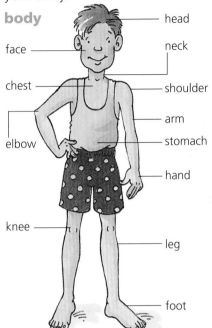

body — head
face — neck
chest — shoulder
elbow — arm
— stomach
— hand
knee — leg
— foot

boil
boils boiling boiled

1 When water **boils**, it becomes very hot. There are bubbles in the water and steam rises from it.

2 When you **boil** food, you cook it in boiling water.

bone
bones

Your **bones** are the hard parts inside your body. Skeletons are made of bones.

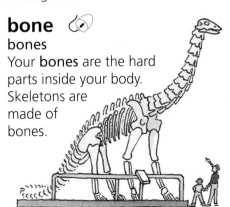

bonfire
bonfires

A **bonfire** is a fire that is lit outdoors.

book
books

A **book** is a group of pages fixed inside a cover. The pages can have writing or pictures on them.

book review
book reviews

When you write a **book review**, you say what you think of a book that you have read.

THE VAMPIRE WHO HATED THE DARK

The vampire who hated the dark

This is a very funny book about a timid vampire called Victor.

I like the part when Victor runs away from his shadow, but I think

the picture could be more exciting. My favourite character is Victor's mum because she puts spiders in his soup.

Some children might be frightened by this book, but I really enjoyed it.

boot
boots

A **boot** is a kind of shoe that covers your foot and part of your leg. People wear boots in bad weather.

bored

If you are **bored**, you are annoyed because you have nothing to do.

born

When a baby is **born**, it comes out of its mother.

borrow
borrows borrowing borrowed

If you **borrow** something, someone lets you have it for a short time. *I borrowed Jo's hat.*

both

Both means two together. *Keep both hands on the handlebars.*

bottle
bottles

Bottles hold liquid. They are made from glass or plastic.

bottom
bottoms

1 The **bottom** is the lowest part of something.

2 Your **bottom** is the part of your body that you sit on.

bought

Bought comes from the word
buy. *We always buy mum a
birthday present. Last year, we
bought her some flowers.*

bounce
bounces
bouncing
bounced
When something **bounces**,
it springs back after hitting
another thing. *The ball
bounced off Hannah's head.*

bow
bows
1 A **bow** is a knot with two loops.
You tie your shoelaces in a bow.
2 A **bow** is also a curved piece of
wood with a string stretched from
one end to the other. You use a
bow to shoot arrows.
3 You also use a **bow** to play the
violin. A bow is made from a long
piece of wood with hair stretched
from one end to the other.
● *See* **musical instruments**
on page 74.

bowl
bowls
You use a **bowl** to
hold food or drink.
Bowls are usually round.

box
boxes
You use a **box** to keep things in.
Boxes usually have straight sides.

boy
boys
A **boy** is a male child.

bracelet
bracelets
A **bracelet** is a chain or a band
that you wear round your wrist.
● *See* **jewellery** *on page 59.*

brain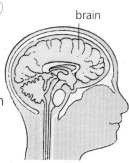
brains
Your **brain**
is inside your
head. You
use your brain
to think and
to make your
body work.

brain

brake
brakes
You use the **brakes** on a car or a
bike to make it slow down or stop.

branch
branches
A **branch** is part of a tree.
Branches grow from the trunk of
a tree.

brave
braver bravest
If you are **brave**, you are not
afraid to do something
frightening. *Ellie was **brave** about
staying in hospital.*

bread
Bread is a food that is made with
flour and baked in an oven.

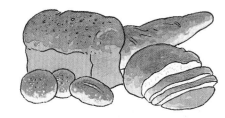

break
breaks breaking broke broken
1 When something **breaks**, it
splits into pieces. *The
mug broke when
Anna dropped it.*
2 When a
machine **breaks**,
it stops working.
*Toby broke
my radio.*

breakfast
breakfasts
Breakfast is the
first meal of the day.

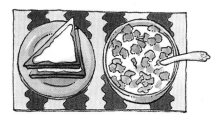

breathe
breathes breathing breathed
When you **breathe**, you suck air
into your body and then let it out
again. You can breathe through
your nose or your mouth.

breeze
breezes
A **breeze** is a gentle wind.

brick
bricks
A **brick** is a block of baked clay.
Bricks are used for building.

bridge
bridges
A **bridge** is something that is built
over a river, a road or a railway
so that people can
get across.

bright
brighter brightest
1 Something that is **bright** gives
out a lot of light. *The Sun is very
bright.*
2 A **bright** colour is strong and
easy to see. *Jemima wore a **bright**
pink jumper.*

brilliant

Something that is **brilliant** is very good. *A brilliant film.*

bring

brings bringing brought

If you **bring** something, you take it with you. *Please bring a packed lunch tomorrow.*

broad

broader broadest

Something that is **broad** is very wide. *A broad river.*

broken

Broken comes from the word **break**. *Toby breaks everything. He has even broken my dad's camera.*

brooch

brooches

A **brooch** is something pretty that you fix with a pin to your clothes.
▲ *rhymes with coach*
● *See* **jewellery** *on page 59.*

brother

brothers

Your **brother** is a boy who has the same mum and dad as you have.

brought

Brought comes from the word **bring**. *Lucy often brings something interesting to school. Last week, she brought her pet snake.*

brown

Brown is a colour. Wood and chocolate are brown.

bruise

bruises

A **bruise** is a purple mark on your skin. You get a bruise when part of your body is hit by something. *Sam has a bruise on his knee where he knocked it.*

brush

brushes

A **brush** has lots of hairs or wires fixed to a handle. You use brushes to tidy your hair, clean your teeth and paint pictures.

bubble

bubbles

A **bubble** is a ball of liquid that is filled with air. There are bubbles in boiling water and in fizzy drinks.

bucket

buckets

You use a **bucket** to hold or carry things. A bucket has a flat bottom, curved sides and a handle.

build

builds building built

If you **build** something, you make it by fixing things together. *Harry is building a model plane.*

building

buildings

A **building** is a place with walls and a roof. Houses, shops, schools and offices are buildings.

built

Built comes from the word **build**. *Hannah won our competition to build the tallest tower. She built one that was three metres high.*

bulb

bulbs

1 A **bulb** is the part of a plant that is under the ground. Flowers, such as daffodils and crocuses, grow from bulbs.
2 A light **bulb** lights up when you turn on a light. Bulbs are made of glass.

bulb

bull

bulls

A **bull** is a male cow. Bulls have horns.

bulldozer

bulldozers

A **bulldozer** is a large machine that moves rocks and soil.

bully

bullies

A **bully** is someone who tries to hurt or frighten other people.

bump

bumps

A **bump** is something round that sticks out. *Osman has a bump on his head.*

bump

bumps bumping bumped

If you **bump** into something, you hit it without meaning to. *Osman bumped into a shelf.*

bunch

bunches

A **bunch** is a group of things. *A bunch of flowers. Bunches of grapes.*

bungalow

bungalows

A **bungalow** is a house with all its rooms on one level.

burglar

burglars

A **burglar** is someone who gets into a building and steals things.

burn

burns burning burned burnt

1 If you **burn** something, you set it on fire. *We burn logs on our fire.*

2 **Burn** also means to damage something with fire or heat. *Humphrey has burnt the toast again.*

3 If you **burn** yourself, you touch something that is hot and get hurt.

burst

bursts bursting burst

When something **bursts**, it breaks apart suddenly. *The bag burst and scattered apples all over the floor.*

bury

buries burying buried

If you **bury** something, you hide it in the ground. *The pirates buried the treasure under a tree.*

bus

buses

A **bus** is a large vehicle that carries lots of people. *Terry travels to school by bus.*

bush

bushes

A **bush** is a plant with lots of branches. Bushes are smaller than trees.

busy

busier busiest

Busy people have a lot of things to do.

butcher

butchers

A **butcher** is someone who sells meat.

butter

Butter is a yellow food that is made from milk. You can spread butter on bread or use it for cooking.

butterfly

butterflies

A **butterfly** is an insect with four large wings.

● *See* **insects** *on page 57.*

button

buttons

A **button** is a small object that is sewn on to clothes. Buttons fit into buttonholes to fasten clothes together.

buy

buys buying bought

When you **buy** something, you pay money so that you can have it. *Kerry bought a kite from the toy shop.*

■ *opposite* **sell**

Cc

cabbage

cabbages

A **cabbage** is a vegetable with a lot of leaves. Cabbages can be green, white or purple.

café

cafés

A **café** is a place with tables and chairs. You buy and eat drinks and snacks in a café.

▲ *say kaf-ay*

cage

cages

A **cage** is a box or a room with bars. Some pets and zoo animals are kept in cages.

cake

cakes

A **cake** is a sweet food that is baked in an oven. Cakes are made with eggs, flour, sugar and butter.

calculator

calculators

A **calculator** is a machine that gives you answers to sums.

calendar

calendars

A **calendar** is a list of all the days, weeks and months in a year. *Victoria marked her birthday on the calendar.*

calf
calves
A **calf** is a baby cow. Baby seals, elephants, giraffes and whales are also called calves.

call
calls calling called
1 If you **call** someone, you shout to them so that they come to you. *Dad **called** us to come inside for dinner.*
2 When you **call** someone something, you give them a name. *Marvin **called** his kitten Pepper.*
3 **Call** also means to telephone. *David **calls** his uncle every week.*

calm
calmer calmest
If you are **calm**, you feel peaceful.

came
Came is from the word **come**. *Henry comes to stay with us every summer. Last year, he **came** in August.*

camel
camels
A **camel** is a large animal with one or two humps on its back. Camels carry people and things across deserts.

camera
cameras
A **camera** is a machine that you use to take photographs.

camp
camps camping camped
When you **camp**, you live in a tent for a short time.

can
cans
A **can** is a metal container with curved sides.

can
could
If you **can** do something, you are able to do it. *Oscar **can** juggle.*

candle
candles
A **candle** is a stick of wax with a string through the middle. When a candle burns, it makes light.

> **Some words that begin** with a "c" sound, such as **kangaroo**, are spelt with a "k".

cannot
If you **cannot** do something, you are not able to do it. *Rebecca **cannot** come.*

canoe
canoes
A **canoe** is a narrow, light boat that you move with paddles.
▲ *say kan-oo*

can't
Can't is a short way of saying **cannot**. *Rebecca **can't** come.*

cap
caps
A **cap** is a soft hat with a peak at the front.

capital
capitals
1 A **capital** is the main city of a country. The leaders of a country work in the capital. *The **capital** of Japan is Tokyo.*
2 A **capital** is a big letter of the alphabet, such as R or Z. You use a capital when you begin a sentence or write a name.

car
cars
A **car** is a machine with four wheels and an engine. People travel from place to place in cars.

car   windscreen

bonnet

tyre

headlight   bumper

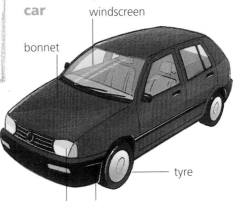

caravan
caravans
A **caravan** is a small home on wheels. Some caravans can be pulled along by a car.

card
cards
1 **Card** is stiff paper.
2 A greetings **card** is a folded piece of stiff paper. It has a picture on the front and a message inside. You send cards to people at special times, such as birthdays.
3 Playing **cards** are pieces of stiff paper with numbers or pictures on them. Playing cards are used to play games.

cardboard
Cardboard is very thick, strong paper. It is used for making boxes.

cardigan
cardigans
A **cardigan** is a knitted jacket. Cardigans fasten at the front.

care
cares caring cared
1 If you **care** for a person or an animal, you look after them. *Harry has two rabbits and he cares for them himself.*
2 If you **care** about something, you think that it is important. *Amy cares about the way she looks.*

careful

If you are **careful**, you think about what you are doing. *Ben was careful not to spill the drinks.*

careless
Someone who is **careless** does not think about what they are doing. *It was careless of Fergus to forget his coat.*

carpet
carpets
A **carpet** is a thick covering for a floor.

carrot
carrots
A **carrot** is a long, orange vegetable that grows under the ground. You can eat carrots raw or cooked.

carry
carries carrying carried
If you **carry** something, you take it somewhere with you. *Jamie carried his bag to the station.*

carton
cartons
Cartons are used to hold food or drink. They are made from card or plastic. *A milk carton.*

cartoon
cartoons
1 A **cartoon** is a film which uses drawings rather than actors.
2 A **cartoon** is also a funny drawing.

case
cases
You use a **case** to hold or carry things. *Timmy keeps his glasses in a case.*

cash
Cash is money in coins and notes.

cassette
cassettes
A **cassette** is a plastic case with a tape inside it. *A video cassette.*

castle
castles
A **castle** is a large building with high walls to keep enemies out. Most castles were built a long time ago.

cat
cats
A **cat** is a furry animal with a long tail. Cats are often kept as pets. Some cats, such as lions and tigers, are large and wild.

catch
catches catching caught
1 When you **catch** something, you take hold of it while it is in the air. *Joseph ran to catch the ball.*
2 If you **catch** a bus or a train, you get on it. *David caught the last bus home.*

caterpillar
caterpillars
A **caterpillar** is a small animal that looks like a worm with lots of short legs. Caterpillars turn into butterflies or moths.

cattle
Cattle is a word for cows and bulls. *We saw some cattle in the fields.*

caught
Caught comes from the word catch. *Joseph ran to catch the ball. He caught it easily.*

cauliflower
cauliflowers
A **cauliflower** is a round vegetable. Cauliflowers have green leaves and a white centre.

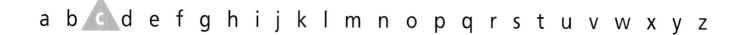
a b **c** d e f g h i j k l m n o p q r s t u v w x y z

For internet links, go to
www.usborne-quicklinks.com
23
cave *to* **ch**ase

cave
caves
A **cave** is a large hole in the side of a cliff or a mountain. There are also caves under the ground.

CD
CDs
CD is short for **compact disc**.

> **Some words that begin** with a "**c**" sound, such as **keep**, **kennel**, **kettle** and **key**, are spelt with a "**k**".

ceiling
ceilings
The **ceiling** is the part of a room that is above your head. Lights hang from ceilings.
▲ say *see*-*ling*

cellar
cellars
A **cellar** is a room under a house.

cement
Cement is a grey powder that is mixed with water and goes very hard when it dries. People use cement to stick bricks together.

centre
centres
The **centre** of something is the middle of it.

century
centuries
A **century** is a period of one hundred years.

cereal
cereals
1 **Cereals** are farm plants such as wheat or rice. Their seeds are used for food.
2 **Cereals** are also foods that you eat for breakfast. Most people eat cereals with milk.

certain
If you are **certain** about something, you are sure about it. *Robert is **certain** that his team will win.*

certificate
certificates
A **certificate** is a piece of paper which says that you have done something. *A cycling **certificate**.*

chain
chains
A **chain** is a row of metal rings that are joined together.

chair
chairs
A **chair** is a seat with four legs and a back. Chairs are made for one person to sit on.

chalk
chalks
Chalk is a soft rock. It can be made into sticks that you use to write and draw.

champion
champions
A **champion** is the winner of a race or a competition.

chance
chances
1 If you have a **chance** to do something, you can do it soon. *Petra has the **chance** to go skiing.*
2 If something happens by **chance**, it has not been planned. *I met my friend by **chance**.*

change
Change is the money that is given back to you when you pay too much for something.

change
changes changing changed
1 When you **change** something, you make it different. *Billy **changed** the date of his party.*
2 When you **change**, you put on different clothes. *Sally **changed** before she went out.*

chapter
chapters
A **chapter** is a part of a book. *That book has 12 **chapters**.*

character
characters
1 A **character** is a person in a story, a film or a play.
2 Your **character** is the sort of person you are.

charge
If someone is in **charge** of something, they look after it. *Mrs Parsnip is in **charge** of our class.*

charge
charges charging charged
If someone **charges** you for something, they ask you to pay money for it.

chart
charts
A **chart** is a picture, a map or a list that shows things clearly.

chase
chases chasing chased
If you **chase** a person or an animal, you run after them and try to catch them. *Finn is **chasing** Felicity.*

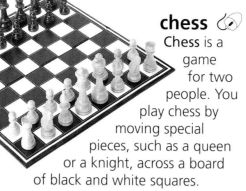

cheap
cheaper cheapest
Something that is **cheap** does not cost much.
■*opposite* expensive

cheat
cheats cheating cheated
If you **cheat**, you break the rules so that you can win or get something that you want.

check
checks
A **check** is a square. *The flag was covered with black and white checks.*

check
checks checking checked
If you **check** something, you make sure that it is right. *Lola checked a spelling in her dictionary.*

cheek
cheeks
Your **cheeks** are the soft sides of your face.

cheerful
Someone who is **cheerful** feels happy or seems happy.

cheese
cheeses
Cheese is a food that is made from milk. Cheese can be hard or soft.

cherry
cherries
A **cherry** is a small, round fruit with a stone in the middle. Cherries can be red, black or yellow.

chess
Chess is a game for two people. You play chess by moving special pieces, such as a queen or a knight, across a board of black and white squares.

chest
chests
1 Your **chest** is the front part of your body between your neck and your waist.
2 A **chest** is a large, strong box that you keep things in. Chests are usually made of wood.

chew
chews chewing chewed
When you **chew** food, you bite it lots of times before you swallow it.

chick
chicks
A **chick** is a very young bird.

chicken
chickens
1 A **chicken** is a bird that is kept on a farm.
2 **Chicken** is also a kind of meat that comes from chickens.

child
children
A **child** is a young boy or girl.

chimney
chimneys
A **chimney** is a wide pipe above a fire that carries smoke out of a building.

chimpanzee
chimpanzees
A **chimpanzee** is an ape with dark fur. Chimpanzees can be quite clever.

chin
chins
Your **chin** is the part of your face below your mouth.

chip
chips
A **chip** is a long, thin piece of potato cooked in hot oil.

chip
chips chipping chipped
If you **chip** something, you break a small piece off it by accident.

chocolate
chocolates
Chocolate is a sweet food that is used to make sweets, cakes and drinks.

choir
choirs
A **choir** is a group of people who sing together.
▲ *say kwire*

choose
chooses choosing chose chosen
If you **choose** something, you pick out the thing that you want. *Dave is choosing a shirt.*

chop
chops chopping chopped
If you **chop** something, you cut it into pieces with a knife or an axe.

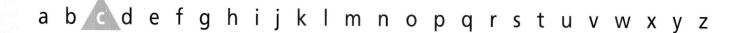

a b **c** d e f g h i j k l m n o p q r s t u v w x y z

chosen

Chosen comes from the word **choose**. *Robbie is allowed to choose what we will do. He has chosen a trip to the fair.*

chunk

chunks

A **chunk** is a thick piece of something. *A chunk of cheese.*

> **Some words that begin** with a "c" sound, such as **kick**, **king**, **kiss** and **kitchen**, are spelt with a "k".

cinema

cinemas

A **cinema** is a place where people go to watch films.

circle

circles

A **circle** is a round shape.
● *See* **shapes** *on page 106.*

circus

circuses

A **circus** is a show that is held in a big tent. Clowns do tricks in circuses.

city

cities

A **city** is a very big place where many people live and work. Cities are larger than towns.

clap

claps clapping clapped

When you **clap**, you make a loud noise by slapping your hands together. People clap to show that they have enjoyed something, such as a play or a concert.

class

classes

A **class** is a group of people who are taught together. *We are in Mrs Parsnip's class at school.*

classroom

classrooms

A **classroom** is a room in a school where children have lessons.

claw

claws

A **claw** is one of the sharp, curved nails on the feet of some birds and animals. Eagles, crocodiles and cats have claws.

clay

Clay is a kind of earth. When clay is wet, it can be made into different shapes. When it dries or is baked, it becomes hard. *Kate made a pot out of clay.*

clean

cleans cleaning cleaned

When you **clean** something, you take the dirt off it. *Pete needs to clean his boots.*

clean

cleaner cleanest

Something that is **clean** does not have any dirt on it. *Marcus wore a clean shirt to go to the party.*
■ *opposite* **dirty**

clear

clearer clearest

1 If a thing is **clear**, you can see through it. *Clear plastic.*
2 Something that is **clear** is easy to understand. *The instructions were clear and easy to follow.*

clever

cleverer cleverest

Someone who is **clever** finds it easy to learn and to understand things. *Josie is clever at maths.*

cliff

cliffs

A **cliff** is a hill with one very steep side. You often see cliffs near the edge of the sea.

climb

climbs climbing climbed

When you **climb** something, you move up it. People sometimes use their hands and feet to climb.

cloak

cloaks

A **cloak** is a loose coat without sleeves.

clock

clocks

A **clock** is a machine that shows you what time it is.

close

closes closing closed

If you **close** something, you shut it. *Close the door behind you.*
▲ *say* **kloze**
■ *opposite* **open**

close

closer closest

If something is **close**, it is near. *Stay close to me.*
▲ *say* **kloze**

cloth
cloths
1 **Cloth** is material that is used to make clothes and curtains.
2 A **cloth** is a piece of material that you use to wipe up a mess.

clothes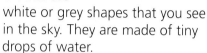
Clothes are things that you wear, such as shirts, socks and trousers.

cloud
clouds
Clouds are white or grey shapes that you see in the sky. They are made of tiny drops of water.

clown
clowns
A **clown** is someone who makes people laugh. Clowns wear funny clothes and do tricks.

club
clubs
A **club** is a group of people who meet together because they enjoy doing the same thing. *Ali has joined a computer **club**.*

clue
clues
A **clue** is something that helps you to find the answer to a question. *The police need some **clues** to help them find the burglar.*

clumsy
clumsier clumsiest
Clumsy people are not very careful about the way they move and often knock things over.

clutch
clutches clutching clutched
If you **clutch** something, you hold on to it tightly. *Fleur **clutched** her friend's arm to stop herself falling.*

coach
coaches
1 A **coach** is a large vehicle that carries a lot of people. Coaches are often used for long journeys.
2 A **coach** is also someone who teaches you to play a sport.

coal
Coal is a black rock that is found under the ground. It makes heat when you burn it.

coast
coasts
The coast is the land next to the sea.

coat
coats
1 A **coat** is a piece of clothing that you wear over your other clothes. Coats have long sleeves and are usually made from thick material.
2 An animal's **coat** is the fur or hair that covers its body. *Fido has a long, thick **coat**.*

cobweb
cobwebs
A **cobweb** is a very thin net that a spider makes. Spiders use their cobwebs to catch insects.

cockerel
cockerels
A **cockerel** is a male chicken. The short name for cockerel is cock.

coin
coins
A **coin** is a round, flat piece of metal. Coins are used as money.

cold
colds
When you have a **cold**, you have a sore throat and you cough and sneeze a lot.

cold
colder coldest
1 If something is **cold**, it is not hot. *A **cold** drink.*
■ *opposite* hot
2 If the weather is **cold**, the temperature is low. *It was so **cold** that Jim shivered.*
■ *opposite* hot

collar
collars
1 The **collar** of a shirt or a jacket is the part of it that fits round your neck.
2 A **collar** is also a band that goes round the neck of a dog or a cat.

collect
collects collecting collected
1 When you **collect** things, you put them together.
2 If you **collect** someone, you take them from a place. *Dad **collected** me from school.*

college
colleges
A **college** is a place where people can learn after they have left school.

colour
colours
Red, yellow and blue are the main **colours**. You can make other colours by mixing the main ones.

colours

yellow

blue

red

orange

green

pink

purple

brown

white

black

comb
combs
A **comb** is a flat piece of plastic or metal with very thin teeth. You use a comb to tidy your hair.

come
comes coming came come
When you **come** to a person or a thing, you move towards them. *Come here so that I can hear you.*

comfortable
If something is **comfortable**, it feels good. *A comfortable chair.*

comic
comics
A **comic** is a magazine with stories told in pictures.

common
commoner commonest
Things that are **common** are ordinary and you see lots of them. *Computers are common in schools.*

compact disc
compact discs
A **compact disc** is a round piece of plastic with music or information stored on it. Compact discs are also called CDs. *Wayne is listening to his new compact disc.*

compare
compares comparing compared
When you **compare** two things, you look at them carefully to see if they are the same or different. *Maisie compared the two dresses to decide which she liked best.*

compass
compasses
1 A **compass** is something that shows you which way you are facing. A compass has a needle which always points north.

2 A **compass** is also a kind of tool that you use to draw a circle.

competition
competitions
When you take part in a **competition**, you try to do better than other people. *I came first in the swimming competition.*

complete
completes completing completed
When you **complete** something, you finish it. *Alice completed her homework and went out to play.*

complete
Something that is **complete** does not have anything missing. *Amy checked to make sure that the jigsaw puzzle was complete.*

computer
computers
A **computer** is a machine that stores words, pictures and numbers. Computers can work things out very quickly. *Jake loves playing games on his computer.*

computer

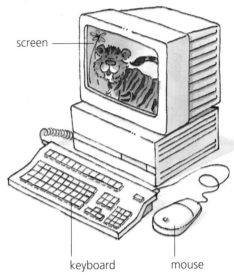

screen

keyboard   mouse

concentrate
concentrates concentrating concentrated
When you **concentrate** on something, you think hard about it. *Akil is concentrating on his game of chess.*

concert
concerts
When people give a **concert**, they play music or sing to an audience.

concrete
Concrete is a mixture of cement, small stones, sand and water. It becomes very hard when it dries. Concrete is used for building.

A B **C** D E F G H I J K L M N O P Q R S T U V W X Y Z

confuse
confuses confusing confused
If someone **confuses** you, they make it hard for you to understand something. *Geraldine confused me with her long words.*

connect
connects connecting connected
If you **connect** two things, you join them together. *Ed connected the computer to the printer.*

consonant
consonants
A **consonant** is any letter of the alphabet except the vowels a, e, i, o and u. B and f are consonants.

contain
contains containing contained
1 If a box **contains** something, it has that thing inside it.
2 If a book **contains** some stories, the stories are in the book.

container
containers
A **container** is something that you use to keep things in. Boxes, bags and baskets are all containers.

continue
continues continuing continued
If you **continue** doing something, you keep on doing it.

control
controls
controlling
controlled
When you **control** something, you make it do what you want. *Arthur can control his toy car.*

conversation
conversations
When two people have a **conversation**, they talk to each other.

cook
cooks cooking cooked
When you **cook** food, you heat it until it is ready to eat.

cool
cooler coolest
Something that is **cool** feels quite cold. *A cool breeze.*

copy
copies
A **copy** is a thing that looks the same as something else. *Jamila liked the painting so much that she made a copy of it.*

copy
copies copying copied
If you **copy** someone, you do the same as they do. *Fergus is copying the way his dad walks.*

cord
cords
Cord is a type of string. Some bags have a cord around the top that you pull to close the bag.

corner
corners
A **corner** is a place where two sides join together. *We met at the the corner of the field.*

correct
If something is **correct**, it does not have any mistakes in it.

correct
corrects correcting corrected
1 When teachers **correct** your work, they check to see if there are any mistakes in it.
2 If you **correct** something, you make it right where it was wrong.

corridor
corridors
A **corridor** is a long passage inside a building or a train.

cost
costs costing cost
If something **costs** a certain amount of money, you can buy it for that much. *How much does that hat cost?*

costume
costumes
A **costume** is a set of clothes that you wear to make yourself look different. *Freddie wore a bear costume for the school play.*

cot
cots
A **cot** is a bed for a baby. Cots have high sides so that the baby cannot fall out.

cottage
cottages
A **cottage** is a small house. You usually see cottages in the country.

cotton
1 **Cotton** is a material that is used to make clothes. Cotton comes from the cotton plant.
2 **Cotton** is also thread that you use to sew.

a b c d e f g h i j k l m n o p q r s t u v w x y z
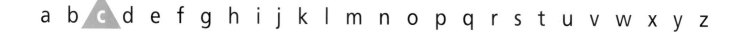

cough
coughs coughing coughed
When you **cough**, you force air out of your throat with a sudden, loud noise. You often cough when you have a cold.
▲ *rhymes with off*

could
Could comes from the word **can**. *Lewis can juggle with four balls. Last month, he could only juggle with three.*

couldn't
Couldn't is a short way of saying **could not**. *Sebastian couldn't swim before he had lessons.*

count
counts counting counted
1 When you **count**, you say numbers one after the other.
2 When you **count** a number of things, you add them up to find out how many there are. *I have counted all the jigsaw pieces.*

counter
counters
1 A **counter** is a long table in a shop. Someone stands behind the counter and serves you.
2 A **counter** is also a small piece of plastic that you use in some games.

country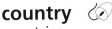
countries
1 A **country** is a part of the world with its own people and laws.
2 The **country** is the land outside towns and cities. There are fields, woods and farms in the country.

cousin
cousins
Your **cousin** is the son or daughter of your aunt or uncle.

cover
covers covering covered
If you **cover** something, you put something else over it. *Monica covered the cake with icing.*

cow
cows
A **cow** is a large farm animal. Cows are kept for their meat and their milk.

crab
crabs
A **crab** is a creature with a hard shell that lives in the sea. Crabs have ten legs. Their front legs have large claws called pincers.

crab
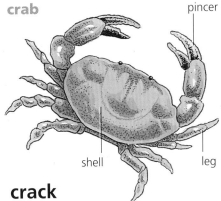
pincer
shell   leg

crack
cracks
A **crack** is a line that shows where something has broken. *This mug has a crack in it.*

crane
cranes
A **crane** is a tall machine that lifts heavy loads.
crane
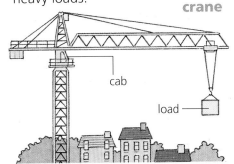
cab
load

crash
crashes
A **crash** is a sudden loud noise. *The plates fell to the ground with a crash.*

crash
crashes crashing crashed
When something **crashes**, it hits something else and makes a sudden loud noise. *The car crashed into a tree.*

crawl
crawls crawling crawled
When you **crawl**, you move around on your hands and knees. *Jemima crawled under the table to hide.*

crayon
crayons
A **crayon** is a coloured pencil. Some crayons are made from wax.

cream
Cream is the thick part of milk. You can use cream in cooking or pour it over puddings and fruit.

creature
creatures
A **creature** is anything that moves and breathes. Horses, lizards, fish, birds and insects are all creatures.

creep
creeps creeping crept
If you **creep** somewhere, you move very slowly and quietly. *Guy crept past his sleeping brother.*

crew
crews
A **crew** is a group of people who work together on a boat or a plane.

cricket

Cricket is a game played by two teams with a bat and a ball. The players have to hit the ball and run up and down the pitch.

cried

Cried comes from the word **cry**. *Pattie began to cry. She cried for half an hour.*

crocodile
crocodiles

A **crocodile** is a reptile that lives in rivers in hot countries. Crocodiles have sharp teeth, short legs and a long tail.

crop
crops

Crops are grown in fields and used for food. Wheat, potatoes and rice are crops.

cross
crosses

A **cross** is a sign. It looks like x or +.

cross
crosses crossing crossed

When you **cross** a road, you go from one side of it to the other.

cross
crosser crossest

If you are **cross**, you are not pleased about something and you feel angry.

> Some other words for **cross** are **angry**, **annoyed**, **irritated** and **furious**.

crossword
crosswords

A **crossword** is a word puzzle with clues. You work out the answer to a clue, then write the word in squares on the puzzle.

ACROSS

1 When you travel by plane, you ____.
3 The colour of the sky on a sunny day.
6 A colour and a fruit.
8 Clothes for your hands.
12 A drop of water from your eye.
13 An animal that you keep at home.
14 When you put two numbers together, you ____.

DOWN

1 Once a tadpole, now a ____.
2 A toy on a string.
4 Not on time.
5 Rain and snow are types of ____.
7 A bird's home.
9 One of the edges of your mouth.
10 Someone who looks after sick animals.
11 Difficult or not soft.

crowd
crowds

A **crowd** is a large group of people. *A football crowd.*

crown
crowns

A **crown** is a special kind of hat made from gold, silver and jewels. Kings and queens wear crowns.

cruel
crueller cruellest

Cruel people are unkind and often hurt other people or animals.

crumb
crumbs

A **crumb** is a very small piece of dry food. *Cake crumbs.*

crust
crusts

The **crust** is the hard part on the outside of a pie or a loaf of bread. *Nathan never eats his crusts.*

a b **c** d e f g h i j k l m n o p q r s t u v w x y z

For Internet links, go to
www.usborne-quicklinks.com
31
cry *to* **da**nce

cry
cries crying cried
When you **cry**, tears come from your eyes. People cry when they are sad or hurt.

cube
cubes
A **cube** is a solid shape with six square sides. *A dice is a* **cube**.
● See **shapes** on page 106.

cucumber
cucumbers
A **cucumber** is a long, green vegetable that you eat in salads.

cuddle
cuddles cuddling cuddled
When you **cuddle** someone, you hold them closely in your arms.

cuff
cuffs
A **cuff** is the part of a shirt that fastens round your wrist.

cup
cups
You drink from a **cup**. Cups are usually round and have a handle on one side.

cupboard
cupboards
A **cupboard** is a piece of furniture in which you keep things. *Biff put his toys in the* **cupboard**.

curious
If you are **curious** about something, you want to find out about it. *Edward was* **curious** *about the parcel.*

curl
curls
A **curl** is a piece of hair that is curved. *Sophie has beautiful* **curls**.

curtain
curtains
A **curtain** is a piece of material that you pull across a window to cover it.

curve
curves
A **curve** is a line that bends.

cushion
cushions
A **cushion** is a kind of pillow. You use cushions to make sofas and chairs more comfortable.

customer
customers
A **customer** is someone who buys something in a shop.

cut
cuts cutting cut
1 If you **cut** something, you use a knife or a pair of scissors to divide it into pieces.
2 When you **cut** yourself, something sharp pushes through your skin and makes you bleed.

cycle
cycles
Cycle is short for **bicycle**.

Dd

dad
dads
Dad is a name for your father.

daily
If something happens **daily**, it happens every day. *Jacob practises the piano* **daily**.

dairy
dairies
A **dairy** is a place where milk is put into bottles or cartons. Food made from milk, such as cheese and yogurt, also comes from dairies.

daisy
daisies
A **daisy** is a flower with white petals and a yellow centre.

damage
damages damaging damaged
If you **damage** something, you break it or spoil it.

damp
damper dampest
Something that is **damp** is a little bit wet. *The dew has made the grass* **damp**.

dance
dances dancing danced
When you **dance**, you move your body to music.

danger
Danger is something that could happen to hurt you.

dangerous
If something is **dangerous**, it can hurt or kill you.

dare
dares daring dared
If you **dare** to do something, you are brave enough to do it. *Peter dared to jump into the river.*

dark
darker darkest
1 When it is **dark**, there is no light or very little light.
2 **Dark** colours are not pale. *Dark blue.*
■ *opposite* **light**

date
dates
When someone asks you what **date** it is, you tell them the day and the month. *The date today is 20th June.*

daughter
daughters
A **daughter** is somebody's female child.

day
days
1 A **day** starts and ends at midnight. There are 24 hours in a day.
2 **Day** is the time when it is light outside. *We've been out all day.*

dead
If a person, an animal or a plant is **dead**, they are no longer living.
■ *opposite* **alive**

deaf
Deaf people cannot hear at all or cannot hear very well.

dear
dearer dearest
1 If someone is **dear** to you, you love them. *A dear friend.*
2 You use the word **dear** when you begin a letter. *Dear Mrs Bott.*

decide
decides deciding decided
When you **decide** to do something, you make up your mind to do it. *Pippa decided to wear her purple shorts.*

deck
decks
A **deck** is a floor on a boat or a ship.

decorate
decorates decorating decorated
1 When you **decorate** something, you add things to it to make it look prettier. *Milly decorated the hall for her party.*
2 If you **decorate** a room, you paint it or put wallpaper on its walls.

deep
deeper deepest
Something that is **deep** goes down a long way. *A deep well.*
■ *opposite* **shallow**

deer
deer
A **deer** is an animal with four legs and brown fur. Deer live in forests and can run very fast. Male deer have big horns called antlers.

delicious
Food or drink that is **delicious** tastes or smells very good.

deliver
delivers delivering delivered
If you **deliver** something, you take it to somebody. *The postman delivered a parcel for Jill.*

dentist
dentists
A **dentist** is someone who takes care of your teeth.

depth
depths
The **depth** of a thing is the distance between its top and its bottom. *We measured the depth of the pool.*

describe
describes describing described
When you **describe** something, you say what it is like. *Tristan described his new house to me.*

desert
deserts
A **desert** is a large piece of land where very few plants grow. Deserts are very dry and are often covered with sand.

deserve
deserves deserving deserved
If you **deserve** a thing, you earn it by doing something. *Tim deserves a rest after all his hard work.*

desk
desks
A **desk** is a kind of table that you sit at to write.

dessert
desserts
A **dessert** is a sweet food that you eat at the end of a meal. *Tanya chose ice cream for dessert.*

destroy
destroys destroying destroyed
Destroy means to damage something so badly that it cannot be mended. *The storm destroyed our garden shed.*

diagram
diagrams
A **diagram** is a drawing that shows something in a clear and simple way.

diamond
diamonds
1 A **diamond** is a jewel. Diamonds are clear and shiny.
2 A **diamond** is also a shape with four sides.
● *See* **shapes** *on page 106.*

diary
diaries
A **diary** is a book in which you write down things that happen to you each day.

dice
A **dice** is a cube with a different number of spots on each side. You use a dice in some games.

dictionary
dictionaries
A **dictionary** is a book of words. Dictionaries tell you what words mean and show you how to spell them.

didn't
Didn't is a short way of saying did not. *Matthew didn't like the film.*

die
dies dying died
When a person, an animal or a plant **dies**, they stop living.

different
If a thing is **different**, it is not the same as something else.

difficult
If something is **difficult**, you need to try hard to do it.
■ *opposite* **easy**

dig
digs digging dug
When you **dig**, you make a hole in the ground. You usually dig with a spade.

dinner
dinners
Dinner is a name for the biggest meal of the day.

dinosaur
dinosaurs
Dinosaurs were reptiles that lived millions of years ago. Some dinosaurs were very big and fierce.

dinosaurs

direction
directions
1 A **direction** is the way that you go to get to a place. *The station is in this direction.*
2 **Directions** are pictures and words that show you how to do something. *These directions show you how to make a kite.*

dirty
dirtier dirtiest
If something is **dirty**, it has mud, food or other marks on it. *Dirty boots.*
■ *opposite* **clean**

diplodocus

stegosaurus

tyrannosaurus rex

triceratops

A B C D E F G H I J K L M N O P Q R S T U V W X Y Z

disagree

disagrees disagreeing disagreed
If you **disagree** with someone, you do not think the same as they do about something. *We disagreed about the film. Jake thought it was good, but I thought it was awful.*

disappear

disappears disappearing disappeared
If something **disappears**, you cannot see it any more. *The Sun disappeared behind a cloud.*
■ *opposite* **appear**

disappointed

If you are **disappointed**, you are sad because something has not happened. *Jo was disappointed that her friend couldn't come.*

disaster

disasters
A **disaster** is something terrible that happens.

disco

discos
A **disco** is a party with music for dancing. There are often flashing lights at discos.

discover

discovers discovering discovered
When you **discover** something, you find out about it for the first time. *Megan discovered that her friend had been lying.*

discuss

discusses discussing discussed
When you **discuss** something, you talk about it with someone else. *We discussed which way we would go home.*

disease

diseases
A **disease** is something that makes you ill. Measles is a disease.

disguise

disguises
A **disguise** is something that you wear to make you look like someone else.

dish

dishes
You put food in a **dish**. Dishes are usually round.

dishonest

Someone who is **dishonest** does not tell the truth.
■ *opposite* **honest**

dishwasher

dishwashers
A **dishwasher** is a machine that washes and dries plates and dishes.

disk

disks
A **disk** is a flat piece of metal and plastic that stores information from a computer.

disobey

disobeys disobeying disobeyed
If you **disobey** someone, you do not do what they tell you to do.
■ *opposite* **obey**

display

displays
A **display** is a group of things that have been arranged for people to look at. *An art display.*

dissolve

dissolves dissolving dissolved
When a tablet **dissolves** in water, it mixes so well with water that you cannot separate them easily.

distance

distances
The **distance** between two things is the space between them. *We measured the distance between the two tables.*

disturb

disturbs disturbing disturbed
If you **disturb** someone, you stop them doing something for a short time. *Roger keeps disturbing me when I am trying to read.*

dive

dives diving dived
When you **dive** into water, you jump in head first, with your arms stretched out in front of you.

divide

divides dividing divided
1 When you **divide** something, you make it into smaller pieces. *Ed divided the cake into six pieces.*
2 When you **divide** numbers, you find out how many times one number goes into another. *Hans divided 12 by 2.*

$$12 \div 2 = 6$$

doctor

doctors
A **doctor** is someone who helps sick people to get better.

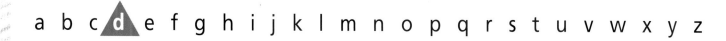
a b c **d** e f g h i j k l m n o p q r s t u v w x y z

doesn't

Doesn't is a short way of saying does not. *Eva doesn't like cold weather.*

dog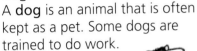

dogs

A **dog** is an animal that is often kept as a pet. Some dogs are trained to do work.

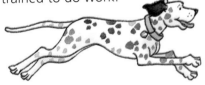

doll

dolls

A **doll** is a toy that looks like a person.

don't

Don't is a short way of saying do not. *I don't like strawberries.*

door

doors

You use a **door** to get into a building, a room or a cupboard.

double

Double means twice as big. *Your lolly is double the size of mine.*

doubt

doubts doubting doubted

If you **doubt** something, you are not sure about it. *I doubted if Simon's story was true.*

▲ *say dowt*

doughnut

doughnuts

A **doughnut** is a small cake which is covered with sugar. Doughnuts sometimes have jam inside them.

down

When something moves **down**, it goes from a higher place to a lower place. *We rode our bikes down the hill.*

■ opposite up

drag

drags dragging dragged

If you **drag** something, you pull it along the ground. *Davina dragged her sledge up the hill.*

donkey

donkeys

A **donkey** is an animal that looks like a small horse. Donkeys have long ears and a furry coat.

dragon

dragons

A **dragon** is a fire-breathing monster that you read about in stories. Dragons have wings and a long tail.

drain

drains

A **drain** is a pipe that carries away liquids.

drama

When you do **drama**, you act and make up plays.

drank

Drank comes from the word drink. *Leo likes to drink milk. He drank three glasses this morning.*

draughts

Draughts is a game for two people. You play draughts by moving counters across a board of black and white squares.

▲ *rhymes with rafts*

draw

draws
drawing
drew drawn

When you **draw**, you use pencils or crayons to make a picture.

drawer

drawers

A **drawer** is a box that slides in and out of a piece of furniture. You use drawers to keep things in.

drawing

drawings

A **drawing** is a picture made with pencils or crayons.

drawn

Drawn comes from the word draw. *Laura likes to draw. She has drawn a picture of a house.*

dream

dreams

A **dream** is a story that you see and hear while you are sleeping.

dress
dresses
A **dress** looks like a skirt and a top joined together. Women and girls wear dresses.

dress
dresses dressing dressed
When you **dress**, you put on your clothes. *Billy dressed quickly.*

drew
Drew comes from the word **draw**. *We all had to draw our favourite food. I **drew** a bowl of ice cream.*

dried
Dried comes from the word **dry**. *We hung the clothes outside to dry. They had **dried** by lunch time.*

drill
drills
A **drill** is a tool that makes holes in hard surfaces.

drink
drinks drinking drank drunk
When you **drink**, you swallow liquid.

drip
drips dripping dripped
When something **drips**, drops of liquid fall from it. *The tap is dripping.*

drive
drives driving drove driven
When someone **drives** a vehicle, they make it go somewhere.

drop
drops
A **drop** is a tiny amount of liquid. *Drops of rain.*

drop
drops dropping dropped
If you **drop** something, you let it fall. *Denise **dropped** her dinner on the floor.*

drove
Drove comes from the word **drive**. *Joseph drives a truck. He **drove** thousands of miles last month.*

drown
drowns drowning drowned
If someone **drowns**, they die because they are under water and cannot breathe.

drum
drums
A **drum** is a hollow musical instrument with a thin skin stretched over each end. You hit the skin with sticks or with your hands.

drunk
Drunk comes from the word **drink**. *Amelia drinks tea all the time. She has **drunk** six cups already today.*

dry
dries drying dried
When you **dry** something, you take water out of it or off it. *Miranda is **drying** the dishes.*

dry
drier driest
Something that is **dry** does not have any water in it or on it.
■ *opposite* **wet**

duck
ducks
A **duck** is a bird that can swim. Ducks have short legs and can dive under water.

dug
Dug comes from the word **dig**. *The pirates began to dig. They **dug** a hole to hide their treasure.*

dull
duller dullest
1 A **dull** colour is not very bright.
2 Something that is **dull** is not very interesting. *A **dull** book.*

dungeon
dungeons
A **dungeon** is a prison under the ground. Dungeons are usually found in castles.

dust
Dust looks like powder and is made up of tiny, dry pieces of dirt. *The furniture was covered in **dust**.*

dustbin
dustbins
A **dustbin** is a large container with a lid. You put your rubbish in a dustbin.

duvet
duvets
A **duvet** is a thick cover for a bed. Duvets are filled with feathers or other soft material.
▲ *say **doo-vay***

dying
Dying comes from the word **die**. *Plants die if you do not give them water. Our plants were **dying** when we returned from holiday.*

Ee

each

Each means every one. *Hal gave each puppy a name. The roses cost £1 each.*

eager

If you are **eager** to do something, you really want to do it. *Alexander is eager to learn to play the guitar.*

eagle

eagles
An **eagle** is a large bird with a curved beak and sharp claws. Eagles hunt small animals for food.

ear

ears
Your **ears** are the parts of your body that you use to hear.

early

earlier earliest
1 If you arrive **early**, you arrive before the time that you were expected. *Sally was early because her watch was wrong.*
2 **Early** also means near the beginning of something. *We set off early in the morning.*
■ *opposite* **late**

earn

earns earning earned
If you **earn** money, you work to get it. *Clare earned some money by working in her uncle's garden.*

earth

1 Plants grow in the **earth**.
2 The **Earth** is the planet that we live on.

earthquake

earthquakes
When there is an **earthquake**, the ground shakes and buildings often fall down.

east

East is a direction. The Sun rises in the east.

easy

easier easiest
If something is **easy**, you do not have to try hard to do it.
■ *opposite* **difficult**

eat

eats eating ate eaten
When you **eat**, you chew and swallow food. *Simon is eating his lunch.*

echo

echoes
An **echo** is a sound that you hear again and again. *Our voices made echoes in the cave.*
▲ *say ek-oh*

edge

edges
An **edge** is the place where something ends. *The glass fell off the edge of the table. We played at the edge of the pond.*

effect

effects
An **effect** is a thing that happens because of something else. *This spell has the amazing effect of turning a prince into a frog.*

effort

If you put **effort** into something, you try very hard at it. *Misha has put a lot of effort into her project.*

egg

eggs
Eggs contain young birds or insects which break out when they are ready to be born. People often eat hens' eggs.

either

Either means one or the other. *You can have either an apple or an orange.*

elbow

elbows
Your **elbow** is the joint in the middle of your arm, where it bends.

electricity

Electricity is a kind of energy that makes light and heat. Electricity is also used to make machines work.

elephant

elephants
An **elephant** is a large animal with a long trunk and two tusks.

emergency
emergencies
An **emergency** is a serious problem that happens suddenly. You need to act quickly in an emergency.

empty
emptier emptiest
If something is **empty**, there is nothing inside it.
■ *opposite* full

encyclopedia
encyclopedias
An **encyclopedia** is a book that contains information about many different subjects.

end
ends
The **end** of something is its last part. *The **end** of the story. The **end** of the train.*

end
ends ending ended
If you **end** something, you finish it. *Simone **ended** the argument by walking out.*

enemy
enemies
Your **enemy** is someone who hates you and wants to hurt you.

energy
1 When you have **energy**, you have the strength to do things. *Mo is full of energy.*

2 **Energy** is also the power that makes machines work and produces heat and light.

engine
engines
1 An **engine** is a machine that makes things move or work. Cars, planes and ships have engines.

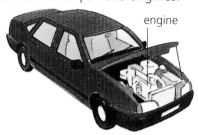
engine

2 An **engine** is also the front part of a train that pulls it along.

enjoy
enjoys enjoying enjoyed
If you **enjoy** something, you like doing it. *Akiko **enjoys** skating.*

enormous
Something that is **enormous** is very big. *Whales are **enormous**.*

enough
If you have **enough** of something, you have as much as you need. *Have you had **enough** lunch?*

enter
enters entering entered
When you **enter** a place, you go into it.

entrance
entrances
An **entrance** is a way into a place. *We searched for the **entrance** to the secret passage.*
■ *opposite* exit

envelope
envelopes
An **envelope** is a paper cover for a letter or a card.

environment
Your **environment** is the land, water and air around you.

equal
Things that are **equal** are the same. *Mix **equal** amounts of blue and red paint.*

equipment
Equipment is a name for the things that you need to do a job. *Bowls and saucepans are types of cooking **equipment**.*

escape
escapes escaping escaped
When people or animals **escape**, they get away from somewhere. *The kitten **escaped** between Jo's legs.*

especially
Especially means more than anything else. *I **especially** liked the purple hat.*

even
1 An **even** number is a number that you reach when you count in twos. *2, 4, 6 and 8 are **even** numbers.*
■ *opposite* odd
2 Something that is **even** is flat or smooth. *An **even** road.*

evening
evenings
The **evening** is the part of the day between the afternoon and the night.

ever
Ever means at any time. *Have you **ever** been skating?*

every
Every means all the people or things in a group. *Matthew tried **every** chocolate in the box.*

evil

Someone who is **evil** is very bad and likes to hurt other people.

exactly

Exactly means just right. *The dress fitted me **exactly**.*

example

examples

An **example** is a thing that you use to show what similar things are like. *Vikram showed us an **example** of his drawings.*

excellent

Something that is **excellent** is very good. *An **excellent** book.*

except

Except means leaving out someone or something. *Everyone except Oliver enjoyed the film.*

excited

If you are **excited** about something, it makes you feel very happy and you keep thinking about it.

excuse

excuses

An **excuse** is a reason that you give for doing or for not doing something. *Hannah is often late for school, but she always has an **excuse**.*

exercise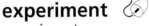

exercises

1 You do **exercise** to keep you fit and strong. Running and swimming are kinds of exercise.
2 An **exercise** is a short piece of work that helps you to practise something that you have learnt. *A maths **exercise**.*

exit

exits

An **exit** is a way out of a place.
◼ *opposite* **entrance**

expect

expects expecting expected

If you **expect** something, you think that it will happen.

expensive

Something that is **expensive** costs a lot of money.
◼ *opposite* **cheap**

experiment

experiments

An **experiment** is a test that you do to find out something.

Experiment

We tested lots of things to see if they would float. First we guessed which ones would float. Then we put them in water and watched carefully. The chart shows the results.

object	floats	sinks
cork	✓	
marble		✓
crayon		

explain

explains explaining explained

When you **explain** something, you talk about it clearly so that other people will understand it. *Madhur explained to her brother how the engine worked.*

explode

explodes exploding exploded

When something **explodes**, it bursts apart with a very loud noise.

explore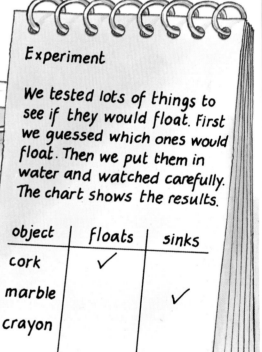

explores exploring explored

If you **explore** a place, you look around it for the first time. *The girls **explored** the old house.*

extinct

If a plant or an animal is **extinct**, there are no more of them alive. *Dodos are extinct.*

extra

Extra means more than the usual amount. *Ellen had an **extra** cake.*

extraordinary

Something that is **extraordinary** is very unusual.

eye

eyes

Your **eyes** are the parts of your body that you use to see.

Ff

face
faces
Your **face** is the front part of your head.

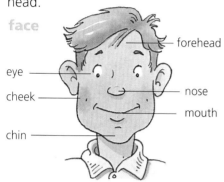

face

forehead
eye
cheek
nose
mouth
chin

face
faces facing faced
If you **face** something, you look towards it. *Turn to **face** the wall.*

fact
facts
A **fact** is something that is true.

factory
factories
A **factory** is a place where things are made by machines or people. *Cars are made in **factories**.*

fade
fades fading faded
When a colour **fades**, it gets paler. *My red shirt has **faded** to pink.*

fail
fails failing failed
If you **fail** at something, you do not succeed in doing it. *James searched for his watch, but **failed** to find it.*

faint
fainter faintest
If a noise or a colour is **faint**, it is not very strong. *The baby bird made a **faint** sound.*

fair
fairs
A **fair** is a place with rides and games where people go to have fun.

fair
fairer fairest
1 If something is **fair**, it seems right. *If I have a ride, it is **fair** that you should have one too.*
2 **Fair** hair is pale yellow.

fairy
fairies
In stories, a **fairy** is a tiny person with wings. Fairies can make magic things happen.

fall
falls falling fell fallen
When someone **falls**, they suddenly go down to the ground. *Leo **fell** off the ladder.*

false
falser falsest
Something that is **false** is not real or not true.

family
families
A **family** is a group of people who live together. Families are usually made up of parents and children.

famous
Someone who is **famous** is very well known.

fan
fans
A **fan** pushes air on to you so that you keep cool. Fans can work by electricity, or you can wave them with your hand.

fancy dress
When you wear **fancy dress**, you put on special clothes to make you look like someone different.

fang
fangs
A **fang** is a long, pointed tooth.

far
farther farthest
Far means a long way. *My friend has moved **far** away.*
■ *opposite* **near**

a b c d e **f** g h i j k l m n o p q r s t u v w x y z

fare
fares
A **fare** is the money that you pay to travel on a bus or a train.

farm
farms
A **farm** is an area of land where farmers grow crops and keep animals.

fast
faster fastest
Something that is **fast** can move quickly. *A fast car.*
■ *opposite* slow

> **Some other words for**
> fast are **quick**, **swift**, **rapid**
> and **speedy**.

fasten
fastens fastening fastened
When you **fasten** something, you close it up. *Jenny fastened her jacket. Jamal fastened his seat belt.*

fat
fatter fattest
A person or an animal that is **fat** has a big, round body. *Our cat is very fat because he eats so much.*
■ *opposite* thin

father
fathers
A **father** is a man who has a child.

fault
If something bad is your **fault**, you made it happen. *It's Ben's fault that we are late because he walks so slowly.*

favour
favours
If you do someone a **favour**, you do something helpful for them.

favourite
Your **favourite** thing is the one you like most of all. *Polly is wearing her favourite cap.*

fear
Fear is the feeling that you have when you think that something bad might happen. *Jon shook with fear as he entered the cave.*

feast
feasts
A **feast** is a large and special meal made for lots of people.

feather
feathers
Feathers cover a bird's body and keep it warm. They are very soft and light.

feed
feeds feeding fed
When you **feed** a person or an animal, you give them food. *Vicky never forgets to feed her cat.*

feel
feels feeling felt
1 When you **feel** something, you touch it to find out more about it. *Feel how cold my hands are!*
2 If you **feel** happy or sad, warm or cold, that is how you are at the time. *Michelle felt upset when Kevin left.*

feeling
feelings
A **feeling** tells you how you are or what mood you are in. *Leo had a sudden feeling of fear.*

fell
Fell comes from the word **fall**. *Joe often falls when he climbs trees. He fell last year and broke his leg.*

felt
Felt is a thick, soft cloth.

felt
Felt comes from the word **feel**. *I feel all right today, but yesterday I felt terrible.*

female
A **female** person or animal belongs to the sex that can have babies.

fence
fences
A **fence** is a wall made from wood or wire. *A garden fence.*

ferry
ferries
A **ferry** is a boat that takes people and cars across water.
● *See* **boats** *on page 16.*

festival
festivals
A **festival** is a special day or a special time of the year.

fetch
fetches fetching fetched
When you **fetch** something, you go to get it and then bring it back. *Katherine **fetched** her book from upstairs.*

fever
If you have a **fever**, you have a high temperature because you are ill.

few
If you have a **few** of something, you do not have many of them. *Don't eat my sweets. I've only got a **few**.*

field
fields
A **field** is a piece of land where people grow crops or keep animals.

fierce
fiercer fiercest
A **fierce** animal is wild and could hurt you. *A **fierce** tiger.*

fight
fights fighting fought
When people **fight**, they try to hurt each other. *The knights **fought** with swords.*

fill
fills filling filled
When you **fill** something, you put so much into it that you cannot add any more.

film
films
1 When you watch a **film**, you see moving pictures on a screen. Films are shown in cinemas or on television.
2 A **film** is also a roll of special plastic that you use in a camera to take photographs.

filthy
filthier filthiest
Something that is **filthy** is very dirty. *Sam's boots are **filthy**.*

fin
fins
A **fin** is a thin, flat part that sticks out of a fish's body. Fins help fish to swim.

find
finds finding found
When you **find** something that you have lost, you see where it is. *Megan **found** her hamster under the bed.*

fine
1 When the weather is **fine**, it is dry and often sunny.
2 If you feel **fine**, you feel well and happy.

finger
fingers
Your **fingers** are the long, thin parts at the end of your hand. You have five fingers on each hand. One of these fingers is called a thumb.

finish
finishes finishing finished
When you **finish** something, you come to the end of it. *Cath quickly **finished** her lunch.*

fire
fires
A **fire** is very hot and bright and is made by burning something. *The firefighters tried to put out the fire.*

fire engine
fire engines
A **fire engine** is a kind of truck which carries equipment to put out fires. Firefighters travel to a fire in a fire engine.

firefighter
firefighters
A **firefighter** is someone whose job is to put out fires.

firework
fireworks
When someone lights a **firework**, it makes loud noises and flashes of coloured light.

firm
firmer firmest
Something that is **firm** does not move or change shape easily. *A **firm** mattress.*

first
If someone is **first**, they come before everyone else. *Henry came **first** in the race.*

first aid

First aid is the help that you give people who are hurt or ill before a doctor sees them.

fish

fish *or* fishes

A **fish** is a creature that lives in water. Fish use their gills to breathe under water.

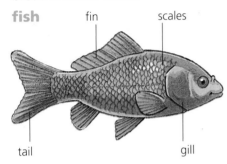

fish   fin   scales   tail   gill

fist

fists

When you make a **fist**, you close your hand tightly.

fit

fits fitting fitted

If clothes **fit** you, they are the right size for you.

fit

fitter fittest

Someone who is **fit** is healthy. *Jessie runs every day to keep* **fit**.

fix

fixes fixing fixed

1 When you **fix** something to another thing, you join them together. *Dad has* **fixed** *the shelf to the wall.*
2 If you **fix** something that is broken, you mend it. *Luke is* **fixing** *our radio.*

fizzy

fizzier fizziest

A **fizzy** drink has lots of bubbles in it.

flag

flags

A **flag** is a special piece of cloth with coloured shapes on it. Each country of the world has its own flag.

flame

flames

A **flame** is the hot, bright light that comes from something that is burning. *A candle* **flame**.

flash

flashes

A **flash** is a bright light that starts and stops suddenly. *A* **flash** *of lightning.*

flask

flasks

You use a **flask** to carry drinks. Some flasks keep drinks hot or cold. *Kirsty took some orange juice in a* **flask** *for her lunch.*

flat

flats

A **flat** is a home on one floor of a building.

flat

flatter flattest

Something that is **flat** does not curve or have any bumps. *A* **flat** *roof. A* **flat** *lawn.*

flavour

flavours

The **flavour** of something is what it tastes like. *What* **flavour** *is your ice cream?*

flew

Flew comes from the word **fly**. *I am going out to fly my new kite. Yesterday, I* **flew** *it all afternoon.*

float

floats floating floated

1 When something **floats** in water, it stays on the surface.
2 When something **floats** through the air, it moves slowly above the ground. *The balloon* **floated** *over the trees.*

flock

flocks

A **flock** is the name for a group of sheep or birds. *A* **flock** *of geese.*

flood

floods

A **flood** is a large amount of water that covers ground which is usually dry. *We had a* **flood** *in our town.*

floor

floors

1 A **floor** is the part of a room that you walk on.
2 A **floor** is also all the rooms on one level of a building. *Jonah's flat is on the second* **floor**.

flour

Flour is a powder made from wheat. You use flour to make bread and cakes.

flower
flowers
A **flower** is part of a plant. Flowers are often brightly coloured and some flowers smell nice.

flown
Flown comes from the word **fly**. *The baby birds are learning to fly. Some have* **flown** *away already.*

flu
If you have **flu**, your body aches and you have a high temperature.

fly
flies
A **fly** is an insect with very thin, clear wings.
● See **insects** *on page 57.*

fly
flies flying flew flown
When something **flies**, it moves through the air.

foal
foals
A **foal** is a baby horse.

fog
Fog is thick cloud that is close to the ground. When there is a fog, you cannot see very far.

fold
folds folding folded
When you **fold** something, you bend one part of it over another part. *Samantha* **folded** *the paper.*

folder
folders
You keep pieces of paper in a **folder**. *A homework* **folder**.

follow
follows following followed
1 If you **follow** someone, you go behind them.
2 If something **follows** another thing, it happens after it. *Summer* **follows** *spring.*

fond
fonder fondest
If you are **fond** of someone, you like them very much.

Some words that begin with an "f" sound, like **phone** and **photograph**, are spelt "ph".

---

food
Food is what people eat to help them stay healthy and grow.

foot
feet
Your **foot** is the part of your body at the end of your leg. You stand on your feet.

foot

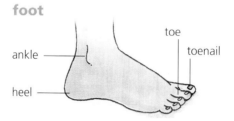

ankle

heel

toe

toenail

football
footballs
1 **Football** is a game played by two teams on a pitch. Each team tries to score goals by kicking a ball into a net.
2 A **football** is the ball used in football games.

footprint
footprints
A **footprint** is a mark made by a foot or a shoe.

forehead
foreheads
Your **forehead** is the part of your face above your eyebrows.

foreign
Something that is **foreign** comes from another country. *Katy collects* **foreign** *coins.*

forest
forests
A **forest** is a place where many trees grow close together.

forever
If something goes on **forever**, it never ends. *The story seemed to go on* **forever**.

forgave
Forgave comes from the word **forgive**. *It is kind to forgive people. Ellie* **forgave** *her sister for ruining her book.*

forget
forgets forgetting forgot forgotten
If you **forget** something, you do not remember it.

forgive
forgives forgiving forgave forgiven
When you **forgive** someone, you stop being angry with them.

forgotten

Forgotten comes from the word **forget**. *Martin might forget to bring his book. He's **forgotten** it before.*

fork

forks

You use a **fork** to eat with. Forks have a handle and three or four sharp points.

fortnight

fortnights

A **fortnight** is two weeks. There are 14 days in a fortnight.

forwards

If you move **forwards**, you move ahead or towards the front. *Gary ran **forwards** to catch the ball.*
■ *opposite* **backwards**

fossil

fossils

A **fossil** is what is left of an animal or a plant that lived millions of years ago. Fossils are found in rocks.

foster

fosters fostering fostered

When people **foster** a child, the child comes to live with them for a short time and becomes part of their family.

fought

Fought comes from the word **fight**. *My brothers often fight. Yesterday, they **fought** over who would have the last biscuit.*

found

Found comes from the word **find**. *Mum asked me to find my book. I **found** it under the bed.*

fountain

fountains

A **fountain** is a spray of water that is pushed up into the air.

fox

foxes

A **fox** is a wild animal that looks like a dog. Foxes have pointed ears and very thick tails.

fraction

fractions

A **fraction** is a part of a whole thing. Halves and quarters are fractions.

frame

frames

A **frame** fits around the edge of something, like a picture or a window.

freckles

Freckles are light brown spots on your skin. *Ginger's nose is covered with **freckles**.*

free

1 If something is **free**, you do not have to pay any money for it. *A **free** gift.*
2 If a person or an animal is **free**, they can go where they like or do what they like.

freeze

freezes freezing froze frozen

When water **freezes**, it becomes so cold that it changes into ice.

freezer

freezers

A **freezer** is a machine that keeps food very cold so that it does not go bad.

fresh

fresher freshest

1 If food is **fresh**, it has just been made or picked. *Fresh fruit.*
2 **Fresh** water is not salty. The water in rivers, lakes and ponds is fresh.

fridge

fridges

A **fridge** is a machine that keeps food and drinks cool. Fridge is short for refrigerator.

fried

Fried food has been cooked in hot oil or butter.

friend

friends

A **friend** is someone you like and who likes you. *Ricky and his **friend** enjoy relaxing together.*

friendly
friendlier friendliest
A **friendly** person likes to meet other people and is kind to them.

frightening
If something is **frightening**, it makes you feel afraid.
A frightening story.

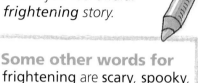

Some other words for frightening are **scary**, **spooky**, **terrifying** and **petrifying**.

fringe
fringes
Your **fringe** is the hair that hangs down over your forehead.

frog
frogs
A **frog** is a small creature with smooth skin, large eyes and strong back legs that it uses for jumping. Frogs live near water.

front
fronts
The **front** of something is the part that faces ahead or comes first.
*Karen sat at the **front** of the bus.*
■ *opposite* **back**

frost
Frost is a thin layer of ice that covers things outside when it is very cold.
*Gregory scraped the **frost** off the windscreen.*

frown
frowns frowning frowned
When you **frown**, you push your eyebrows together and wrinkle your forehead. You frown because you are cross or because you are thinking about something.

frozen
1 If a pond is **frozen**, the surface of the water has changed into ice.

2 **Frozen** food is kept very cold so that it does not go bad.

fruit
fruits
A **fruit** is the part of a plant that holds the seeds. Many fruits are good to eat.

fry
fries frying fried
When you **fry** food, you cook it in hot oil or butter. *Dad **fried** an egg for his lunch.*

full
fuller fullest
If something is **full**, it cannot hold any more.
*The jar is **full** of biscuits.*
■ *opposite* **empty**

fumes
Fumes are gases that smell bad and make you cough.
*Cars make **fumes**.*

fun
When you have **fun**, you have a good time and you are happy.

funny
funnier funniest
1 If something is **funny**, it makes you laugh. *A **funny** joke.*
2 **Funny** also means strange or peculiar. *We heard a **funny** noise coming from the attic.*

fur
Fur is the soft hair that covers some animals' bodies.
*Polar bears have thick, white **fur**.*

furious
If you are **furious**, you are very angry. *Sophie was **furious** that her watch had been stolen.*
▲ *say **fyoor-ee-uss***

furniture
Furniture is the name for all the big things, like tables, chairs and beds, that people have in their houses. *When we moved house, we bought some new **furniture**.*

fuss
fusses fussing fussed
If you **fuss** about something, you worry about it more than you need to. *Mum is always **fussing** about my clothes.*

future
The **future** is the time that has not happened yet. *In the **future**, we might have robots to look after us.*

Gg

gallop
gallops galloping galloped
When a horse
gallops, it runs
very fast.

game
games
1 A **game** is something that you play. Games have rules. Football and draughts are games.

2 You also play a **game** when you pretend to be someone else. *We played a **game** of explorers.*

gang
gangs
A **gang** is a group of people who do things together.

gap
gaps
A **gap** is a space between two things. *Marcus has a **gap** between his two front teeth.*

garage
garages
1 A **garage** is a building where a car is kept.
2 A **garage** is also a place where people buy petrol and get their cars mended.

garden
gardens
A **garden** is a piece of land near a house where people grow grass, flowers and other plants.

gas
gases
A **gas** is very light and usually cannot be seen. The air is made of gases. Some gases burn easily and are used in ovens and fires.

gate
gates
A **gate** is a kind of door in a fence, a wall or a hedge.

gave
Gave comes from the word **give**.
I want to give my dad a present.
*Last year, I only **gave** him a card.*

generous
A **generous** person likes to help people and give them things.
*It was very **generous** of Uncle Bill to buy me a bicycle.*

gentle
gentler gentlest
When you are **gentle**, you are careful and kind. *Rosa is **gentle** with her baby sister.*

gerbil
gerbils
A **gerbil** is a small, furry animal with long back legs. People often keep gerbils as pets.

germ
germs
A **germ** is a tiny living thing that travels in the air and can make you ill. You need a microscope to see germs. *Cover your mouth when you cough, so that you don't spread your **germs**.*

ghost
ghosts
A **ghost** is a person who has died who some people think they can see.

giant
giants
A **giant** is a very tall person that you read about in stories.
*The **giant** bent down and picked up the man.*

gift
gifts
A **gift** is something special that you give to someone.
*We wrapped Yasmin's **gift** carefully.*

giggle
giggles giggling giggled
When you **giggle**, you laugh in a silly way. *Alice kept **giggling** at her dad's new shorts.*

A B C D E F **G** H I J K L M N O P Q R S T U V W X Y Z

giraffe
giraffes

A **giraffe** is an animal with a very long neck and long legs. Giraffes live in herds and are the tallest animals in the world.

girl
girls

A **girl** is a female child or a young woman.

give
gives giving gave given

When you **give** something to someone, you let them have it to keep. *Posy loves giving presents to her friends.*

glad
When you are **glad**, you are pleased and happy about something. *I'm glad that you are feeling better.*

glass
glasses

1 **Glass** is a hard material that you can see through. Windows and bottles are made of glass. It is quite easy to break glass.

2 A **glass** is a container that you drink from. Glasses are made from glass. *Dan poured some juice into his glass.*

glasses
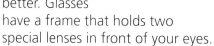
People wear **glasses** to help them see better. Glasses have a frame that holds two special lenses in front of your eyes.

globe
globes

A **globe** is a round model of the Earth. Globes are often fixed to a stand so that you can spin them. *Alexander is trying to find New Zealand on his globe.*

glove
gloves

Gloves are clothes that you wear on your hands to keep them warm.

glue
Glue is a thick liquid that you use to stick things together. You use glue to make things or to mend things that are broken.

go
goes going went gone

1 **Go** means to move from one place to another. *Let's go home.*

2 **Go** also means that something will happen. *Betsy is going to be eight next week.*

goal
goals

You score a **goal** by kicking, hitting or throwing a ball into a net.

goat
goats

A **goat** is an animal with horns and a short tail. Most goats have beards.

gold
Gold is a yellow metal that is very valuable. *A gold ring.*

goldfish
goldfish

A **goldfish** is a small, orange fish. People often keep goldfish as pets.

gone
Gone comes from the word **go**. *Let's go to the park. The others have gone there already.*

good
better best

1 If something is **good**, you like it. *A good book.*
■ *opposite* **bad**

> Some other words for **good** are **marvellous, fantastic, great** and **terrific**.

2 **Good** children behave well.
■ *opposite* **bad**
3 **Good** work has been done well.
■ *opposite* **bad**

goodbye
You say **goodbye** when someone goes away.

goose
geese

A **goose** is a large bird with a long neck. Geese can swim and fly.

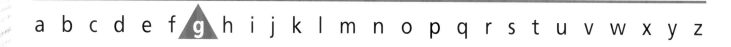

grab
grabs grabbing grabbed
If you **grab** something, you pick it up in a quick, rough way. *Ginger grabbed his bag and ran.*

gradual
If something is **gradual**, it happens slowly. *A gradual change.*

grain
grains
1 A **grain** of something, such as sand or salt, is a tiny piece of it.
2 A **grain** is also a seed. *A grain of rice. A grain of wheat.*

grandfather
grandfathers
Your **grandfather** is the father of your mother or your father. Children often call their grandfather grandpa or grandad.

grandmother
grandmothers
Your **grandmother** is the mother of your mother or your father. Children often call their grandmother granny or grandma.

grape
grapes
A **grape** is a small, round fruit that grows in bunches. Grapes are green or purple.

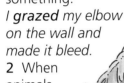

grapefruit
grapefruits
A **grapefruit** is a large, round fruit with a thick skin. It is yellow or pink and has a sharp taste.

grass
grasses
Grass is a plant with thin, green leaves. Grass grows in fields and gardens.

grateful
If you are **grateful**, you want to thank someone for something that they have done.

gravy
Gravy is a hot, brown sauce that you eat with meat.

graze
grazes grazing grazed
1 If you **graze** your skin, you scrape it against something. *I grazed my elbow on the wall and made it bleed.*
2 When animals **graze**, they eat grass that is growing in a field.

great
greater greatest
1 **Great** means large. *The trees grew to a great height.*
2 **Great** also means important. *A great leader.*
3 **Great** also means very good. *We had a great holiday.*

greedy
greedier greediest
Greedy people want more of something than they need. *Augustus was so greedy that he ate five bowls of ice cream.*

green
Green is the colour that you make when you mix blue and yellow. Grass is green.

greenhouse
greenhouses
A **greenhouse** is a building with a glass roof and walls. People grow plants in greenhouses.

grew
Grew comes from the word **grow**. *Sunflowers grow very fast. Last week, ours grew five centimetres.*

grey
Grey is the colour that you make when you mix black and white. Rain clouds are grey.

grin
grins
A **grin** is a big smile.

grip
grips gripping gripped
If you **grip** something, you hold on to it tightly. *Gregory gripped the baseball bat.*

ground
The **ground** is the surface that you walk on outside.

group
groups
A **group** is a number of people or things that are together or are the same in some way.

grow

grows growing
grew grown
When something
grows, it gets bigger.

growl

growls growling growled
When a dog **growls**, it makes a
long, low sound in its throat.
*Fido **growled** every time the cat
came near.*

grown

Grown comes from the word
grow. *My auntie is amazed at the
way I grow. She says I have **grown**
five centimetres since the summer.*

grown-up

grown-ups
A **grown-up** is someone who is
no longer a child.

grumble

grumbles grumbling grumbled
If you **grumble**, you keep on
saying that you are not happy or
that you do not like something.

guard

guards guarding guarded
If you **guard** something, you
watch it carefully to keep it safe.

guess

guesses guessing guessed
If you **guess**, you try to think of an
answer to something that you do
not know already. *Sam tried to
guess how many
sweets were in
the jar.*

guest

guests
A **guest** is someone who comes to
visit you. *We have **guests** coming
to dinner tonight.*

guinea pig

guinea pigs
A **guinea pig** is a
small, furry animal
with no tail. People
often keep guinea
pigs as pets.

guitar

guitars
A **guitar** is a
musical
instrument
with strings.
You play
a guitar by
pressing the
strings with
one hand and
pulling them
with the other.

gum

gums
1 Your **gums** are the firm pink
skin around your teeth.
2 **Gum** is a kind of
sweet that you
chew, but do
not swallow.

gun

guns
A **gun** is a weapon
that is used to shoot
something.

gymnastics

Gymnastics are
exercises that you do
to make you fit and
strong. *Jasmine
is practising
gymnastics.*

Hh

habit

habits
A **habit** is something that you do
often, usually without thinking
about it. *Hayley's worst **habit** is
biting her nails.*

had

Had comes from the word **have**.
*We often have fish for dinner. We
had it twice last week.*

hadn't

Hadn't is a short way of saying
had not. *Natasha **hadn't** seen
the film.*

hail

hails hailing
hailed
When it
hails,
small pieces
of frozen rain
fall from the
sky. *It is **hailing**
on my umbrella.*

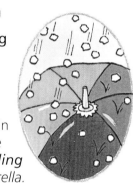

hair

Hair is what grows on your head
and on many animals' bodies.
*Leah has very long **hair**.*

half

halves
A **half** is
one of
two pieces
that are the same
size. *Camilla cut
her apple into
halves.*

hall
halls
1 A **hall** is a room with other rooms coming off it.
2 A **hall** is also a large room that is used for meetings or plays.

halo
haloes
A **halo** is a circle of light around the head of an angel.

hammer
hammers
A **hammer** is a tool that you use for hitting nails. It has a handle and a heavy metal end.
● *See* **tools** *on page 128.*

hamster

hamsters
A **hamster** is a small, furry animal that looks like a mouse. Hamsters
have short tails and store food in their cheeks. They are often kept as pets.

hand

hands
Your **hand** is the part of your body at the end of your arm. You use your hands to hold things.

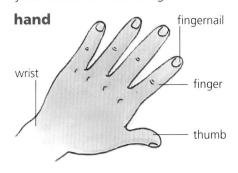

hand
fingernail
wrist
finger
thumb

hand
hands handing handed
If you **hand** something to someone, you give it to them.
*Please **hand** me a brush.*

handbag
handbags
A **handbag** is a bag used to carry money and other small things.

handkerchief
handkerchiefs
A **handkerchief** is a square piece of cloth that you use to wipe your nose.

handle
handles
You use a **handle** to hold something or to move something. *The **handle** on my suitcase is broken. Sophie turned the door **handle** slowly.*

handsome
Men and boys who are **handsome** are good looking.

handwriting

Your **handwriting** is the way that you write letters and words. *Ben has beautiful **handwriting**.*

hang
hangs hanging hung
If you **hang** something up, you fix the top of it to a hook or a knob. *Lucille **hung** up her coat.*

happen
happens happening happened
When something **happens**, it takes place. *What **happens** at the end of the book?*

happy
happier happiest
When you are **happy**, you feel pleased about things.
■ *opposite* **sad**

Some other words for
happy are **glad**, **cheerful**, **pleased** and **delighted**.

harbour

harbours
A **harbour** is a safe place where boats can be tied up.

hard
harder hardest
1 Something that is **hard** is firm and solid. *A **hard** bed.*
■ *opposite* **soft**
2 If something is **hard**, it takes a lot of work to do it or to understand it. ***Hard** sums.*

harmful
If something is **harmful**, it could hurt you or make you ill.

harvest

harvests
Harvest is the time when crops are cut or picked.

has
Has comes from the word **have**. *Adam will have a party for his birthday. He **has** one every year.*

hasn't
Hasn't is a short way of saying **has not**. *Micky hasn't arrived yet.*

hat
hats
A **hat** is something that you wear on your head.

hatch
hatches hatching hatched
When an egg **hatches**, a baby bird or animal breaks out of it.

hate
hates hating hated
If you **hate** something, you do not like it at all. *Mark hates cabbage.*

haunted
If a place is **haunted**, people think that there are ghosts in it.

have
has having had
1 If you **have** something, it is yours. *I have a new bicycle.*
2 When you **have** something, you feel it. *Sarah has a cold. Edward had a shock.*

haven't
Haven't is a short way of saying **have not**. *We haven't any money.*

head
heads
1 Your **head** is the part of your body where your hair, eyes, mouth and nose are. Your brain is inside your head.
2 The **head** of something is the person in charge. *The head of a school.*

heal
heals healing healed
When a cut **heals**, it gets better.

healthy
healthier healthiest
1 A **healthy** person is well and strong.
2 Something that is **healthy** is good for you. *I try to eat healthy food, such as fruit and vegetables.*

heap
heaps
A **heap** is an untidy group of things. *Samir left his clothes in a heap on the floor.*

hear
hears hearing heard
When you **hear**, you notice sounds with your ears.

heart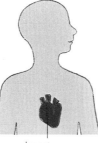
hearts
Your **heart** is the part of your body that pushes blood round your body.

heart

heat
heats heating heated
When you **heat** something, you make it warmer. *Janice heated the soup in a saucepan.*

heavy
heavier heaviest
Something that is **heavy** weighs a lot. *Paul tried to lift the heavy suitcase.*
■ *opposite* **light**

hedge
hedges
A **hedge** is a row of bushes that make a kind of wall. You often see hedges round fields.

heel
heels
Your **heel** is the back part of your foot.

height
heights
Your **height** is how tall you are. *Emma checked Guy's height to see if he had grown.*

held
Held comes from the word **hold**. *Henry offered to hold the ladder for his dad. He held it until his arms ached.*

helicopter
helicopters
A **helicopter** is a small aircraft without wings. It has blades on top that spin around to make it fly or hover.
● *See* **aircraft** *on page 7.*

he'll
He'll is a short way of saying **he will**. *James is finishing his lunch. He'll be here soon.*

hello
You say **hello** when you meet someone.

helmet
helmets
A **helmet** is a hard hat that you wear to protect your head. *Nadya is wearing her bicycle helmet.*

help
helps helping helped
If you **help** someone, you do something for them. *Lauren helped her dad to put up the tent.*

helpful
A **helpful** person likes to help other people.

hen
hens
A **hen** is a female bird that lives on a farm. Hens lay eggs.

herd
herds
A **herd** is a large group of animals. *A herd of elephants.*

here
Here means the place where you are. *I've lived here for six years.*

here's
Here's is a short way of saying **here is**. *Here's today's newspaper.*

herself
Herself means her and nobody else. *Emily has hurt herself.*

he's
He's is a short way of saying **he is**. *I'm waiting for Giles to arrive. He's coming at two o'clock.*

hibernate
hibernates hibernating hibernated
When animals **hibernate**, they sleep through the winter. They hibernate to stay alive when it is cold and there is not much food. Some mice and bears hibernate.

hiccup
hiccups
When you have **hiccups**, you keep making a sudden sound in your throat.

hide
hides hiding hid hidden
1 When you **hide** something, you put it where no one can see it. *Zak hid the present under the bed.*
2 If you **hide** your feelings, you keep them secret. *Rosie hid her disappointment.*

high
higher highest
1 Something that is **high** is a long way from the ground. *A high tower.*
2 **High** also means larger than usual. *High prices.*
3 A **high** voice goes up a long way. Girls and young boys have high voices when they sing.
■ *opposite* **low**

hill
hills
A **hill** is a high piece of land. Hills are not as tall as mountains.

himself
Himself means him and nobody else. *Max has hurt himself.*

hippopotamus
hippopotamuses
A **hippopotamus** is a large animal with short legs and thick skin. Hippopotamuses live near water.

history
History is the story of what has happened in the past.

hit
hits hitting hit
When you **hit** something, you push or knock it very hard. *Rex hit the ball. Peter hit his head.*

hobby
hobbies
A **hobby** is something that you enjoy doing in your spare time. *Jon's hobby is collecting badges.*

A B C D E F G **H** I J K L M N O P Q R S T U V W X Y Z

hold
holds holding held
1 If you **hold** something, you have it in your hands or your arms. *Liz held the kitten gently.*
2 **Hold** also means to have room for something. *This jug holds two litres. The hall holds about two hundred people.*

Some words that begin with an "h" sound, such as **whole**, are spelt **"wh"**.

hole
holes
A **hole** is a gap or a hollow place. *A hole in your trousers. A hole in the ground.*

holiday
holidays
A **holiday** is a time when you do not have to work or go to school. People often spend their holidays away from home.

hollow
Something that is **hollow** has an empty space inside it. *We crawled through the hollow log.*

home
homes
Your **home** is the place where you live. *We are going to stay at home today.*

homework
Homework is work that a teacher gives you to do at home.

honest
Someone who is **honest** tells the truth and can be trusted.
■ *opposite* **dishonest**

honey

Honey is a sweet, sticky liquid that is made by bees. You can eat honey on bread.

hood
hoods
The **hood** of a coat is the part that covers your head. *As soon as it started to rain, Ruth put up her hood.*

hoof
hooves
An animal's **hoof** is the hard part of its foot. Horses, deer and cows have hooves.

hook
hooks
A **hook** is a curved piece of metal or plastic. Some hooks are used for hanging things up. Other hooks are used for catching things, like fish.

hop
hops hopping hopped
1 When you **hop**, you jump on one foot.
2 When birds, rabbits and kangaroos **hop**, they jump forwards with their feet close together.

hope
hopes hoping hoped
If you **hope** for something, you want it to happen and think that it might. *I hope that we'll go to the seaside tomorrow.*

horn
horns
1 A **horn** is one of the hard, pointed bones that grow out of some animals' heads. Goats and bulls have horns.
2 A **horn** is also a musical instrument that you blow.

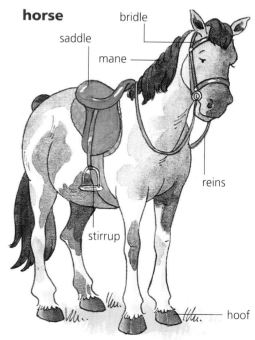
horn

horrible
Something that is **horrible** is awful or frightening. *A horrible lunch. A horrible dream.*

horse
horses
A **horse** is an animal with four legs and a long tail. People ride horses.

horse

bridle
saddle
mane
reins
stirrup
hoof

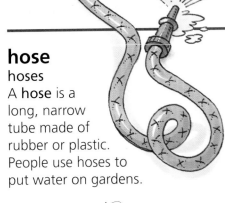

hose
hoses
A **hose** is a long, narrow tube made of rubber or plastic. People use hoses to put water on gardens.

hospital
hospitals
A **hospital** is a building where people who are ill or hurt are looked after. Doctors and nurses work in hospitals.

hot
hotter hottest
Something that is **hot** has a high temperature. *A hot drink.*
■ *opposite* **cold**

hotel
hotels
A **hotel** is a big building with many bedrooms and a restaurant. People pay to stay in hotels when they are away from home.

hour
hours
An **hour** is an amount of time. An hour lasts for 60 minutes. There are 24 hours in a day.

house
houses
A **house** is a building that people live in. *Where is your house?*

hover
hovers
hovering
hovered
When something **hovers**, it stays in one place in the air. *The helicopter hovered over the houses.*

how
1 **How** means in what way. *How do I turn off the computer?*
2 You also use **how** when you ask about an amount. *How much money do you have? How many people are coming to the play?*

hug
hugs hugging hugged
When you **hug** someone, you hold them tightly in your arms. *Gary hugged Mario when he scored the final goal.*

huge
Something **huge** is very big. *Whales are huge.*

human being
human beings
A **human being** is a person. Men, women and children are all human beings.

hump
humps
A **hump** is a big lump. Camels have humps on their backs.

— hump

hung
Hung comes from the word **hang**. *Tim decided to hang up the picture. He hung it in his room.*

hungry
hungrier hungriest
If you are **hungry**, you want to eat something.

hunt
hunts hunting hunted
1 When animals **hunt**, they chase another animal, then kill it and eat it.
2 If you **hunt** for something, you look for it carefully. *Tony hunted everywhere for his other sock.*

hurry
hurries hurrying hurried
When you **hurry**, you do something quickly. *Mary hurried to catch the bus.*

hurt
hurts hurting hurt
If something **hurts** you, you feel pain. *Stephanie's elbow hurt where she had hit it.*

husband
husbands
A woman's **husband** is the man she is married to.

hut
huts
A **hut** is a small house. Huts can be made from wood, mud or grass.

hutch
hutches
A **hutch** is a kind of cage made from wood and wire. People keep rabbits and other small pets in hutches.

I i

ice
Ice is water that has frozen. Ice is very cold and hard. *The surface of the pond was covered with ice.*

iceberg
icebergs
An **iceberg** is a very large piece of ice that floats in the sea.

ice cream
Ice cream is a sweet, frozen food made from milk or cream. There are many different flavours of ice cream.

icicle
icicles
An **icicle** is a long, thin stick of ice. Icicles are made from dripping water which has frozen.

icing
Icing is used to cover cakes. It is made from sugar mixed with water or butter. *Wayne covered the cake with icing.*

I'd
1 **I'd** is a short way of saying **I had**. *I'd already eaten supper by the time William came.*
2 **I'd** is also a short way of saying **I would**. *I'd love to come to your birthday party.*

idea
ideas
An **idea** is something new that you think of. *Richard had lots of ideas for a story.*

identical
If two things are **identical**, they look exactly the same. *Vanessa and Polly are wearing identical hats.*

ill
When you are **ill**, you are not well. *Nicholas was ill, so he had to stay in bed.*

I'll
I'll is a short way of saying **I will**. *I'll be home before it gets dark.*

I'm
I'm is a short way of saying **I am**. *I'm feeling happy today.*

imagine
imagines imagining imagined
If you **imagine** something, you have a picture of it in your mind. *Celia imagined what it would be like to meet a dragon.*

imitate
imitates imitating imitated
If you **imitate** someone, you copy what they do.

immediately
If you do something **immediately**, you do it now. *Go to your room immediately!*

impatient
If someone feels **impatient**, they are annoyed because they have to wait.

important
If something is **important**, it matters a lot. *It is important to clean your teeth every day.*

impossible
If something is **impossible**, it cannot be done. *It is impossible to control the weather.*

improve
improves improving improved
If something **improves**, it gets better. *My cooking has improved.*

in
1 **In** means not outside.
■ opposite **out**
2 **In** also shows when something happens. *I'll be back in an hour.*

increase
increases increasing increased
If something **increases**, it gets bigger.

indoors
If you are **indoors**, you are inside a building.

infant
infants
1 An **infant** is a baby or a very young child.
2 An **infant** is also a schoolchild who is between four and seven years old.

infectious
If a disease is **infectious**, you can catch it from another person. *Measles is* **infectious**.

information
If you ask for **information** about something, you want to know some facts about it. *Robert is looking for* **information** *about swimming classes.*

ingredient
ingredients
An **ingredient** is one of the things that goes into food. *Katy collected all the* **ingredients** *before she started to cook.*

initial
initials
An **initial** is the first letter of a word or a name. *Edward Thompson's* **initials** *are E.T.*

injured
Someone who is **injured** has been hurt.

ink
inks
Ink is a coloured liquid that is used for writing or printing.

insect
insects
An **insect** is a small creature with six legs. Many insects have wings.

insects

inside
1 If something is **inside** a thing, it is in it. *A plum has a stone* **inside** *it.*
2 Inside also means indoors. *We went* **inside** *when it began to rain.*

instead
Instead means in place of something else. *Barry caught the bus* **instead** *of walking home.*

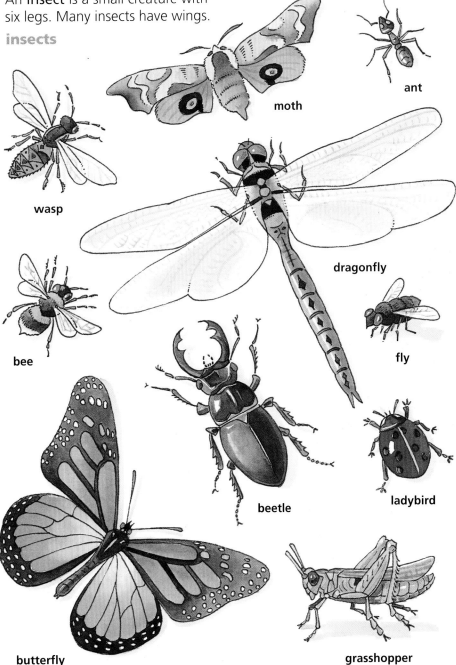

moth

ant

wasp

dragonfly

bee

fly

beetle

ladybird

butterfly

grasshopper

instructions

Instructions are words and pictures that show you how to do something. *Read the **instructions** before you make the model.*

instrument

instruments

1 An **instrument** is something that helps you to do a job. *Doctors and dentists use **instruments**.*
2 An **instrument** is also something that you use to make music. *Pianos, guitars and trumpets are all **instruments**.*

intelligent

An **intelligent** person finds it easy to learn and to understand things.

interesting

If something is **interesting**, you want to know more about it.

interrupt

interrupts interrupting interrupted

If you **interrupt** someone, you stop them in the middle of what they are doing. *Stephen's sister interrupted him while he was listening to a tape.*

invention

inventions

An **invention** is something that nobody has made or thought of before. *My uncle has **invented** a machine that makes his bed.*

invisible

If something is **invisible**, you cannot see it.

invitation

invitations

When you give someone an **invitation**, you ask them to do something with you.

Richard invites Sam to a party on Saturday 4th May at Cherry Tree Cottage Orchard Lane from 2 o'clock to 5 o'clock
Please come dressed as a monster.

iron

irons

1 **Iron** is a strong, hard metal. Gates are often made from iron.
2 People use an **iron** to make their clothes smooth. An iron has a handle and a flat metal bottom that gets hot.

irritable

If someone feels **irritable**, they are cross and easily annoyed. *Sam gets **irritable** when he hasn't had enough sleep.*

island

islands

An **island** is a piece of land with water all around it.

isn't

Isn't is a short way of saying **is not**. *Leon **isn't** coming today.*

itch

itches itching itched

If your skin **itches**, you want to scratch it.

its

Its means belonging to it. *The cat is playing with **its** ball.*

it's

1 **It's** is a short way of saying **it is**. *It's very cold today.*
2 **It's** is also a short way of saying it has. *It's been a long day.*

itself

Itself means it and nothing else. *This machine works by **itself**.*

I've

I've is a short way of saying **I have**. *I've an idea for a story.*

Jj

jacket
jackets
A **jacket** is a short coat.

jam
jams
Jam is a sweet food that is made by boiling fruit and sugar together. *Strawberry jam on toast.*

jar
jars
You use a **jar** to keep things in. Jars are usually made of glass. People buy jam and honey in jars.

jaw
jaws
Your **jaw** is the bone at the bottom of your face. It moves when you speak or eat.

jealous
If you are **jealous**, you are upset because someone has something that you do not have. *Tom felt jealous when Charlie got his new computer.*

jeans
Jeans are trousers that are made from a strong cotton material, called denim.

jelly
jellies
Jelly is a sweet, clear food that wobbles when you move it.

Some words that begin with a "j" sound, such as **generous, gentle, gerbil** and **giant**, are spelt with a "g".

---

jet
jets
A **jet** is an aircraft that travels very fast. Jets have special engines.
● See **aircraft** on page 7.

jewel
jewels
A **jewel** is a very valuable stone. Diamonds are jewels.

jewellery
Jewellery is the name for pretty things, such as bracelets, rings and brooches, that you wear on your body or on your clothes.

jewellery

jigsaw
jigsaws
A **jigsaw** is a picture that has been cut into pieces. You make the picture again by putting the pieces together.

job
jobs
1 A **job** is the work that someone does to earn money. *Mum has a job in an office.*
2 A **job** is also something that needs to be done. *There are lots of jobs to do in the garden.*

join
joins joining joined
1 If you **join** things, you put them together. *Louise joined the pieces of wood to make a table.*
2 If you **join** a club, you become a member of it. *Tessa has joined a gymnastics club.*

joint
joints
A **joint** is a part of your body where two bones meet. Elbows and knees are joints.

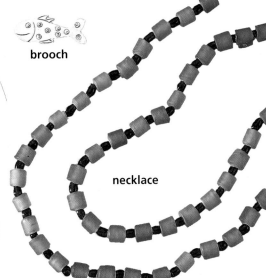

brooch

earrings

necklace

bracelet

ring

joke
jokes
A **joke** is something that you say to make people laugh.

What do you call a cat with eight legs?

An octopuss.

What's orange and sounds like a parrot?

A carrot.

What always follows a crocodile?

Its tail.

What do you find in the middle of India?

The letter "d".

jolly
jollier jolliest
Jolly means happy. *We had a jolly time at the seaside.*

journey
journeys
When you go on a **journey**, you travel from one place to another. *Annabel has a long journey to school.*

jug
jugs
You use a **jug** to hold liquid. You also pour liquid out of a jug.

juggle
juggles juggling juggled
When you **juggle**, you keep things in the air by throwing and catching them, one after the other. *Leo can juggle with balls and clubs.*

juggling ball   juggling club

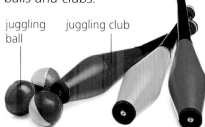

juice
juices
Juice is the liquid that comes from fruit or vegetables. *Apple juice.*

jump
jumps jumping jumped
When you **jump**, you bend your knees and push yourself suddenly into the air. *Leah jumped over the puddle.*

> **Some other words for** **jump** are **leap**, **spring** and **bound**.

jumper
jumpers
A **jumper** is a piece of clothing that covers the top part of your body. Jumpers are often made of wool.

jungle
jungles
A **jungle** is a place in a hot country where many trees and plants grow. Monkeys, parrots and snakes live in jungles.

junior
juniors
A **junior** is a schoolchild who is between eight and eleven years old.

junk
Junk is a name for things that people do not want. Junk is often sold in special shops.

just
1 If something has **just** happened, it happened a short time ago. *Humphrey has just left.*
2 **Just** also means the right amount. *There were just enough seats for everyone.*
3 **Just** also means only. *Don't worry about the noise. It's just the wind in the trees.*

a b c d e f g h i j k l m n o p q r s t u v w x y z

Kk

kangaroo
kangaroos
A **kangaroo** is a large animal that moves about by jumping. Female kangaroos carry their babies in a bag on their stomach, called a pouch.

keen
keener keenest
If you are **keen** to do something, you are excited about it and really want to do it.

keep
keeps keeping kept
1 When you **keep** something, you have it and do not give it away. *Alexander keeps all his old comics.*
2 If you **keep** doing something, you do it again and again. *Mary kept laughing at me.*
3 **Keep** also means to make something stay the same. *Please keep the door closed.*

kennel
kennels
A **kennel** is a small hut that is made for a dog to sleep in.

kept
Kept comes from the word **keep**. *Roger keeps his diary under his bed. He has always kept it there.*

kettle
kettles
You use a **kettle** to boil water. A kettle has a handle and a spout.

key
keys
1 A **key** is a piece of metal that has been cut into a special shape. You use a key to open a lock or to start a car.
2 A **key** is also one of the parts of a piano or a computer that you press to make it work.

kick
kicks kicking kicked
When you **kick** something, you hit it with your foot. *Gary kicked the football into the air.*

kid
kids
1 A **kid** is a young goat.
2 A **kid** is also a child.

kill
kills killing killed
To **kill** means to make something die. *The frost has killed most of the plants.*

kind
kinds
Things of the same **kind** are alike or belong to the same group. *A butterfly is a kind of insect.*

kind
kinder kindest
A **kind** person helps other people. *It was kind of Dot to give us tea.*

king
kings
A **king** is a man who rules a country. Kings come from royal families and are not chosen by the people.

kiss
kisses kissing kissed
When you **kiss** someone, you touch them with your lips.

kitchen
kitchens
A **kitchen** is a room where you cook meals.

kite
kites
A **kite** is a frame covered with paper or cloth with a very long string attached to it. You can fly a kite in the wind.

kitten
kittens
A **kitten** is a very young cat.

knee

knees

Your **knee** is the joint in the middle of your leg, where it bends.

kneel

kneels kneeling knelt

When you **kneel**, you get down on your knees.

knew

Knew comes from the word **know**. *Carrie didn't know about the party, but she **knew** that we were planning something.*

knife

knives

A **knife** is a tool that you use to cut things. Knives have a handle and a metal blade.

knight

knights

A **knight** was a soldier who lived hundreds of years ago. Knights wore armour and fought for their king.

knit

knits
knitting
knitted
When you **knit**, you make clothes from wool, using two long needles. *Meg is **knitting** a scarf.*

knob

knobs

A **knob** is a round handle on a door or a drawer.

knock

knocks
knocking
knocked
1 If you **knock** on something, you hit it. *I **knocked** on the door until someone heard me.*
2 If you **knock** something over, you make it fall. *Freddy has **knocked** over a glass of milk.*

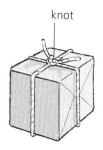

knot

knots

A **knot** is a place where something, such as string, is tied. *Tie a **knot** in the string to make the parcel safe.*

knot

know

knows knowing knew known
1 If you **know** something, you have it in your mind. *Sally **knows** the answers to all the teacher's questions.*
2 If you **know** someone, you have met them before. *I have **known** Adam for years.*

Ll

label

labels

A **label** is a piece of paper or cloth that is attached to something. Clothes often have labels that tell you how to wash them.

lace

Lace is a thin material with lots of holes in it. It is sometimes used to decorate clothes.

laces

Laces are like long pieces of string. You use laces to tie up your shoes.

ladder

ladders

A **ladder** is a set of steps that can be moved around. *Dad used a **ladder** to climb up to the roof.*

lady

ladies

A **lady** is a woman.

ladybird

ladybirds

A **ladybird** is a red or yellow insect with black spots.
● *See **insects** on page 57.*

laid

Laid comes from the word **lay**. *I asked Marcus to lay the clothes on the chair, but he **laid** them on the bed.*

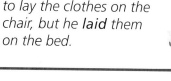

lake
lakes
A **lake** is a large area of water with land all around it.

lamb
lambs
A **lamb** is a young sheep.

lamp
lamps
A **lamp** makes light. Most lamps work by electricity. *Jenny has a lamp by her bed.*

land
Land is the name for the parts of the Earth that are not covered by water.

land
lands landing landed
When a plane **lands**, it comes down from the air to the ground.

landing
landings
A **landing** is the area of a house at the top of the stairs. A landing has other rooms coming off it.

lane
lanes
1 A **lane** is a narrow road, usually in the country.
2 A **lane** is also one of the strips that a wide road is divided into. Motorways usually have three lanes on each side.

language
languages
Language is a name for the words that people use to speak and write to each other. *Fritz can speak three languages.*

lantern
lanterns
A **lantern** is a lamp that you carry. Lanterns sometimes have a candle inside them.

lap
laps
Your **lap** is the top part of your legs, when you are sitting down. *The kitten sat on Daisy's lap.*

lap
laps lapping lapped
When an animal **laps** up a drink, it uses its tongue to drink.

large
larger largest
If something is **large** it takes up a lot of space. *A large room. A large bag of sweets.*

last
1 Something that is **last** comes at the end. *Z is the last letter of the alphabet.*
2 **Last** also means the time before this. *I saw Patrick last week.*

late
later latest
1 If you are **late**, you arrive after the right time. *Tom was late because his watch was wrong.*
2 **Late** also means near the end of something. *We arrived home late in the evening.*
■ *opposite* **early**

laugh
laughs laughing laughed
When you **laugh**, you make sounds which show that you think that something is funny. *Laura always laughs at Carl's jokes.*

law
laws
A **law** is a rule that everyone in a country must obey.

lawn
lawns
A **lawn** is a piece of grass that is kept short. Parks and gardens have lawns.

lay
lays laying laid
1 If you **lay** something somewhere, you put it down carefully. *Tony laid the spoons on the table.*

2 When a bird **lays** an egg, the egg comes out of its body.

lay
Lay comes from the word **lie**. *Sonia decided to lie on the sofa. She lay there for hours.*

layer
layers
A **layer** is something flat that lies above or below something else. *My birthday cake has three layers.*

lazy
lazier laziest
Someone who is **lazy** does not want to do any work. *Jack is too lazy to do his homework.*

A B C D E F G H I J K **L** M N O P Q R S T U V W X Y Z

lead
leads
1 A **lead** is a long strip of leather or a chain that you fix to a dog's collar. You hold the end of the lead and use it to control the dog.
▲ *rhymes with seed*
2 The **lead** in a pencil is the black part that makes a mark.
▲ *rhymes with head*

lead
leads leading led
1 If you **lead** someone to a place, you go with them to show them where it is.
2 If you **lead** a group of people, you are in charge of them.
▲ *rhymes with seed*

leaf
leaves
A **leaf** is one of the thin, flat parts of a plant or a tree. Leaves are usually green but they often change colour in autumn.

leak
leaks leaking leaked
If a container **leaks**, the liquid inside it comes out slowly through a small hole.

lean
leans leaning leant
If something **leans**, it bends to one side. *The tower leant to one side.*

learn
learns learning learnt
When you **learn** something, you get to know it or understand it. *Emma is learning to play tennis.*

least
Least means the smallest amount. *Nobody ate much, but Amanda ate least.*
■ *opposite* **most**

leather
Leather is made from animal skin. It is used to make shoes and bags.

leave
leaves leaving left
1 If you **leave** a place, you go away from it. *I left home early this morning.*
2 When you **leave** something in a place, you let it stay where it is. *I left my jacket at home.*

led
Led comes from the word **lead**. *Rod will lead us up the mountain. He has led us before.*

leek
leeks
A **leek** is a long, white vegetable with green leaves at one end.

left
You have a **left** hand and a right hand. Most people draw with their right hand, but some people use their left hand.
■ *opposite* **right**

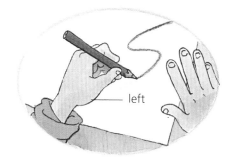
left

left
Left comes from the word **leave**. *We promised to leave before it got dark, so we left at about five o'clock.*

leg
legs
1 Your **legs** are the parts of your body that you use for standing and walking.
2 The **legs** on a table or a chair are the parts that hold it up.

lemon
lemons
A **lemon** is a yellow fruit with a thick skin. Lemons are juicy and have a sharp taste.

lend
lends lending lent
If you **lend** something to someone, you let them have it for a short time. *I lent Zak my pen.*

length
lengths
The **length** of something is how long it is. *Dad measured the length of the wood.*

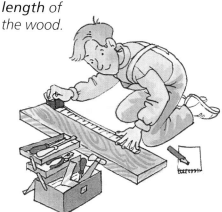

lens
lenses
A **lens** is a special, curved piece of glass or plastic. Lenses are used in glasses and telescopes to make things look clearer or bigger.

lent

Lent comes from the word **lend**.
Bobby often lends me his bicycle.
*He **lent** it to me yesterday.*

leopard

leopards
A **leopard** is
a large wild
cat. Leopards
have dark
yellow fur
with black
spots.
▲ say **lep**-erd

leotard

leotards
A **leotard** is a
piece of clothing
that fits tightly.
You can wear
a leotard when
you dance or
do exercise.
Posy wears a
***leotard** for her*
ballet class.
▲ say **lee**-oh-tard

less

Less means not as much. *I had*
less to eat than my brother.
■ opposite **more**

lesson

lessons
A **lesson** is a period of time when
you are taught something.
*A swimming **lesson**.*

let

lets letting let
If someone **lets** you do something,
they say that you can do it.
*Dad **let** us stay up late.*

let's

Let's is a short way of saying
let us. *Let's go to the cinema.*

letter

letters
1 A **letter** is a sign
that you use to
write words. A, M
and Z are letters.
2 A **letter** is also
a message that
you write on
paper. You
usually put
letters in
envelopes to
post them.

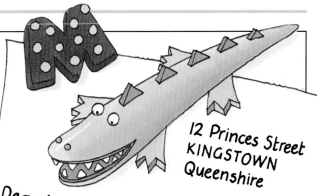

12 Princes Street
KINGSTOWN
Queenshire

20th March

Dear Auntie Brenda
Thank you very much for the
modelling clay that you sent me for my
birthday. The first thing I made was
a letter M for Miranda. Now I'm making
models of all my family. I hope that you
will like the one I made of you.
We're all looking forward to
seeing you soon.

Love from
Miranda.
XXX

lettuce

lettuces
A **lettuce**
is a
vegetable
with large
leaves that
are usually
green. You use
lettuces to make salads.

level

levels
A **level** is a particular height.
Hang the pictures on the wall at
*eye **level**.*

level

Something that is **level** is flat and
smooth. *Football pitches should*
*be **level**.*

library

libraries
A **library** is a place where a lot
of books are kept. You can
borrow books from a library to
read at home.

lick

licks licking licked
If you **lick** something, you move
your tongue along it. *Leila **licked***
her lolly.

lid
lids
A **lid** is the top of a box or other container. To open the container, you lift up the lid or take it off.

lie
lies lying lied
If you **lie**, you say something that is not true.

lie
lies lying lay lain
When you **lie** down, you rest with your body flat on a bed or another surface.

life
lives
Life is the time that someone is alive. *My grandfather had a long and interesting life.*

lift
lifts
A **lift** is a small room that goes up and down. Lifts carry people between floors of a building.

lift
lifts lifting lifted
If you **lift** something, you pick it up. *Jonathan lifted the kitten out of the basket.*

light
lights
1 When there is **light**, you can see things. The Sun, lamps and torches make light.
2 A **light** is something that gives out light, such as a lamp.

light
lights lighting lit
When you **light** a fire, you make it burn. *Mum lit a bonfire.*

light
lighter lightest
1 If it is **light**, you can see things.
■*opposite* **dark**
2 **Light** colours are pale.
■*opposite* **dark**
3 Something that is **light** does not weigh very much.
■*opposite* **heavy**

lighthouse
lighthouses
A **lighthouse** is a tower with a flashing light on top of it. Lighthouses warn ships of danger.

lightning
Lightning is a sudden flash of light in the sky. You sometimes see lightning when there is a storm.

like
likes liking liked
When you **like** something, you enjoy it and think that it is good.

like
If two people are **like** each other, they are the same in some way.

line
lines
1 A **line** is a long, thin mark. *My writing paper has lines printed on it.*
2 A **line** is also a number of people or things in a row. *We stood in a line for the team photograph.*

lion
lions
A **lion** is a large wild cat with light brown fur. Lions live in Africa and India.

lip
lips
Your **lips** are the edges of your mouth.

liquid
liquids
A **liquid** is something that can be poured. Water, oil and fruit juice are all liquids.

list
lists
A **list** is a group of things that are written down one after the other. *A shopping list.*

listen
listens listening listened
When you **listen**, you pay attention to what you are hearing. *Mrs Parsnip asked everybody to* **listen** *carefully.*

lit
Lit comes from the word **light**. *Dad decided to light a fire. He* **lit** *it a long way from the house.*

litter
1 **Litter** is rubbish that has been dropped outside. *The streets were dirty and full of* **litter**.
2 A **litter** is a group of baby animals born at the same time to the same mother. *A* **litter** *of puppies.*

little
1 If something is **little**, it is small.
2 **Little** also means not much. *Martin eats very* **little**.

live
lives living lived
1 Something that **lives** is alive.
2 If you **live** somewhere, your home is there. *Ian lives in London.*

lively
livelier liveliest
Someone who is **lively** has a lot of energy. *Emily is a* **lively** *dancer.*

lizard
lizards
A **lizard** is a small reptile with a long body and a tail. Lizards lay eggs.

load
loads
A **load** is something heavy that has to be moved. *The truck took a* **load** *of sand to the house.*

load

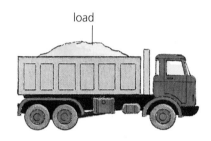

loaf
loaves
A **loaf** is bread that has been baked in a shape.

lobster
lobsters
A **lobster** is a sea creature with a shell and ten legs. You can eat lobsters. Lobsters turn pink when you cook them.
See **sea creatures** *on page 104.*

lock
locks
A **lock** keeps things such as doors and cupboards shut. You need a key to open a lock. *My diary has a* **lock** *on it.*

log
logs
A **log** is a thick piece of wood that has been cut from a tree.

lolly
lollies
A **lolly** is a large sweet or ice cream on a stick.

lonely
lonelier loneliest
If you are **lonely**, you feel unhappy because you are alone.

long
longer longest
1 If something is **long**, one of its ends is far away from the other. *Kamala has very* **long** *hair.*
2 If something takes a **long** time, it takes a lot of time.
■ *opposite* **short**

look
looks looking looked
1 When you **look** at something, you use your eyes to see it. *Jemima is* **looking** *at the view.*
2 If you **look** for something, you try to find it.

loop
loops
A **loop** is a circle made with a rope, a string or a ribbon. *A bow has two* **loops**.

loose
looser loosest
1 Clothes that are **loose** do not fit closely. ***Loose*** *trousers.*
■ *opposite* **tight**
2 Something that is **loose** is not fixed firmly. *A* **loose** *handle.*

lorry
lorries
A **lorry** is a large vehicle that is used for carrying things.

A B C D E F G H I J K **L** M N O P Q R S T U V W X Y Z

lose
loses losing lost
1 If you **lose** something, you do not know where it is. *Justin has lost his watch.*
2 If you **lose** a game or a race, you do not win it.

lot
A **lot** is a large amount. *I had a lot of birthday cards.*

loud
louder loudest
Something that is **loud** makes a lot of noise. *Mum hates loud music.*
■ *opposite* **quiet**

lounge
lounges
A **lounge** is a room where you can sit and relax.

love
loves loving loved
If you **love** someone, you like them very much.

lovely
lovelier loveliest
If something is **lovely**, you really enjoy looking at it or listening to it. *A lovely view. A lovely song.*

low
lower lowest
1 Something that is **low** is not far from the ground. *A low chair.*
2 **Low** also means smaller than usual. *Low prices. A low temperature.*
3 A **low** voice goes down a long way. Most men have low voices.
■ *opposite* **high**

lucky
luckier luckiest
If you are **lucky**, good things happen to you that you have not planned.

luggage
Luggage is the name for the cases and bags that you take with you when you travel.

lump
lumps
1 A **lump** is a piece of something. *A lump of pastry. A lump of coal.*
2 A **lump** is something round that sticks out. *My sauce has lumps in it. Look at this lump on my head!*

lunch
lunches
Lunch is the meal that you eat in the middle of the day. *Francesca always takes a packed lunch to school.*

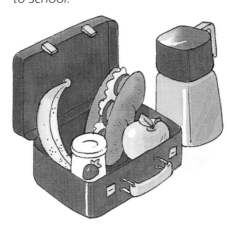

lung
lungs
Your **lungs** are inside your chest. When you breathe, air goes in and out of your lungs.

lung

lying
Lying comes from the word **lie**. *Mum told me never to lie. She was very angry when she heard me lying to Jack.*

Mm

machine
machines
A **machine** is something that does a job. Machines have many moving parts. Cars, computers and cranes are all machines.

made
Made comes from the word **make**. *Fay makes excellent cakes. Yesterday, she made a fruit cake.*

magic
1 In stories, **magic** is the power to make impossible things happen. *By magic, the stone became gold.*
2 **Magic** is also a name for clever tricks that look impossible.

magician
magicians
1 In stories, a **magician** is someone who uses magic to do impossible things.
2 A **magician** is also someone who does surprising tricks. *Dan had a magician at his party.*

magnet
magnets
A **magnet** is a special piece of metal that makes other metals stick to it. Things that are made of iron and steel stick to magnets.

magnifying glass
magnifying glasses
A **magnifying glass** is a glass lens that makes things look bigger.

mail
Mail is a name for the letters and parcels that people post.

main
Main means the biggest or the most important. *The main entrance to the station. The main meal of the day.*

make
makes making made
1 If you **make** something, you put it together. *Terry loves making model planes.*
2 If you **make** something happen, it happens because of what you do. *Sophia teased her brother and made him cry.*

male
A **male** person or animal belongs to the sex that cannot have babies.

mammal
mammals
A **mammal** is an animal that has babies and can feed them with its own milk. Human beings, whales and dogs are all mammals.

man
men
A **man** is an adult, male human being.

manage
manages managing managed
If you **manage** to do something, you do it even though it is difficult. *Patsy managed to swim 20 lengths of the pool.*

manners
Your **manners** are the way that you behave. *Gregory has very good manners. He is always polite and helpful.*

many
Many means a large number. *There are many flowers in our garden.*

map
maps
A **map** is a drawing that shows you where places are. Maps can show roads, rivers and buildings.

marble
marbles
1 A **marble** is a small, glass ball that is used to play a game called marbles.
2 Marble is a hard rock. Statues and buildings can be made from marble.

march
marches marching marched
When soldiers **march**, they all walk together with steps of the same size.

margarine
Margarine is a soft, yellow food like butter. You can spread margarine on bread or use it for cooking.

margin
margins
A **margin** is a long, blank space along the edge of a page.

mark
marks
1 A **mark** is a dirty spot or a stain on something.
2 Teachers give you a **mark** to show how good or bad your work is.

market
markets
A **market** is a place where you can buy things. Markets are often held outdoors.

marmalade
Marmalade is a sweet, sticky food made from oranges or lemons. People often eat marmalade on toast for breakfast.

marry
marries marrying married
When a man and a woman **marry**, they promise to spend their lives together.

A B C D E F G H I J K L **M** N O P Q R S T U V W X Y Z

marsh
marshes
A **marsh** is an area of wet and muddy land. Many birds and animals live on marshes.

mask
masks
A **mask** is something that you wear to cover your face. When you put on fancy dress, you often wear a mask.

mat
mats
1 A **mat** is a small piece of carpet or other material that is used to cover part of a floor.
2 A **mat** is also a small piece of cloth or other material that you put on a table to protect it.

match
matches
1 A **match** is a short, thin stick of wood with a special tip. It produces a flame when you rub its tip on a rough surface.
2 A **match** is a game played by two players or two teams. *A football **match**.*

match
matches matching matched
If two or more things **match**, they look the same in some way. *Jessica's hat, scarf and gloves all **match**. They are exactly the same colour.*

material
materials
1 **Material** is a name for anything used to make something else. Bricks, wood and glass are all building materials.
2 **Material** is also a name for wool, cotton and other kinds of cloth. *Jane's dress is made from thick **material**.*

maths
When you study **maths**, you learn about numbers, amounts and shapes.

matter
matters mattering mattered
If something **matters** to you, you care a lot about it and think that it is important. *It **matters** to me that you come to my party.*

mattress
mattresses
A **mattress** is the thick, soft part of a bed that you lie on. Mattresses often have springs inside them.

may
might
1 If something **may** happen, there is a chance that it will happen. *Susie **may** come round today.*
2 If you **may** do something, you are allowed to do it. *Anna says I **may** use her computer.*

meadow
meadows
A **meadow** is a field of grass.
▲ *say med-oh*

meal
meals
A **meal** is the food that you eat at certain times of the day. Breakfast, lunch and dinner are meals.

mean
means meaning meant
1 When you say what something **means**, you explain it. *William told us what the signs **meant**.*
2 If you **mean** to do something, you plan to do it. *I didn't **mean** to hurt my brother.*

mean
meaner meanest
Someone who is **mean** is not generous or kind.

measles
Measles is an infectious disease. When you have measles, lots of red spots appear on your skin and you have a high temperature.

measure
measures measuring measured
When you **measure** something, you find out how big or how heavy it is.

meat
Meat is a kind of food that comes from animals. Beef, lamb and chicken are types of meat.

medal
medals
Medals are given to people as prizes or rewards. They often look like a coin, hanging from a ribbon.

medicine

medicines
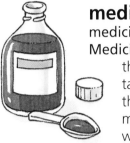
Medicine is a liquid that people take when they are ill to make them well again.

medium
Medium means between big and small in size.

meet
meets meeting met
If you **meet** someone, you both go to the same place at the same time. *I met Lucy outside the museum.*

melt
melts melting melted
When something **melts**, it becomes much warmer and changes into liquid. *My ice lolly melted in the sunshine.*

member
members
If you are a **member** of a group, you are one of the people in it.

memory
You use your **memory** to remember things. If you have a good memory, you remember things. If you have a bad memory, you forget them.

mend
mends mending mended
If you **mend** something that is broken, you put it right so that it can be used again. *Dillon is mending his kite.*

menu
menus
A **menu** is a list of food that you can buy in a restaurant or a café.

mess
If something is a **mess**, it is very untidy and sometimes dirty. *Your bedroom is a mess!*

message
messages
A **message** is a piece of information that you send to someone or leave for someone.

Don't forget your lunch!

met
Met comes from the word **meet**. *The members of the computer club meet every week. Last term, they met on Fridays.*

metal

metals
A **metal** is a hard material that is found in the ground. Metals are used to make things such as machines, vehicles and jewellery. Iron, copper and gold are metals.

microphone
microphones
You use a **microphone** to make your voice sound louder.

microscope
microscopes
A **microscope** makes small things look much bigger, so that you can see and study them. *We looked at leaves and petals through a microscope.*

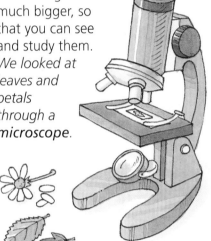

midday
Midday is 12 o'clock in the middle of the day.

middle
middles
1 The **middle** of something is the place that is the same distance away from all its sides. *There is a tree in the middle of our garden.*
2 If you are in the **middle** of something, you have started it and want to finish it. *Alice is in the middle of watching her favourite programme.*

A B C D E F G H I J K L M N O P Q R S T U V W X Y Z

midnight
Midnight is 12 o'clock at night.

might
Might comes from the word may. *We may go out today. Sarah said she might come too.*

milk
Milk is a white liquid that mothers feed to their babies. People often drink cows' milk.

mime
mimes
miming
mimed
When you mime, you act without using any words. *Ella mimed being trapped in a tower.*

mind
minds
Your mind is the part of you that thinks, remembers and imagines.

mine
mines
A mine is a place where things, such as coal or diamonds, are dug out of the ground.

mine
If something is mine, it belongs to me. *Don't touch that chocolate. It's mine!*

minus
Minus means take away. The sign for minus is - . *Ten minus four is six.*

minute
minutes
A minute is an amount of time. A minute lasts for 60 seconds. There are 60 minutes in an hour.

mirror
mirrors
A mirror is a special piece of glass that you can see yourself in. *Nat is looking at himself in the mirror.*

mischievous
Someone who is mischievous is lively and naughty. *The mischievous children helped themselves to the cake.*

miserable
Someone who is miserable feels sad and unhappy. *Robin is miserable because it is raining.*

miss
misses missing missed
1 If you miss someone, you are unhappy because they are not with you.
2 If you miss a train or a bus, you do not manage to catch it.
3 If you miss a ball, you do not manage to catch it or hit it.

mist
Mist is cloud that is close to the ground. When there is a mist, you cannot see very far.

mistake
mistakes
If you make a mistake, you do something wrong.

mix
mixes mixing mixed
When you mix things, you put them together to make one thing. *Joe mixed red and yellow paint to make orange paint.*

mixture
mixtures
A mixture is something that you make by mixing things together. Mud is a mixture of earth and water.

moan
moans moaning moaned
1 If you moan, you make a long, low sound because you are unhappy or hurt.
2 If you moan about something, you say that you are unhappy about it. *Jules was moaning because it was too wet to go outside.*

model
models
A model is a small copy of something. *Jake has a model of a sailing boat inside a bottle.*

moment
moments
A moment is a very short amount of time. *Wait a moment while I shut the door.*

money
Money is the name for the coins and notes that you use to buy things.

a b c d e f g h i j k l **m** n o p q r s t u v w x y z

monkey
monkeys
A **monkey** is an animal with long arms and legs, a very long tail and a furry body. Monkeys live in trees in hot countries.

monster
monsters
In stories, a **monster** is a large, fierce animal or person. Monsters often look very ugly.

month
months
A **month** is a period of about four weeks. There are twelve months in a year. *May and July are **months**.*

mood
moods
Your **mood** is the way that you feel. *Antonia is in a good **mood** because she is on holiday.*

Moon
The **Moon** is the large, bright object that you often see in the sky at night. It takes one month for the Moon to go round the Earth.

more
More means larger in number or size. *My brother ate **more** lunch than I did.*
■ *opposite* less

morning
mornings
The **morning** is the part of the day before midday.

most
Most means the largest amount. *My brother ate more than I did, but my father ate **most** of all.*

moth
moths
A **moth** is an insect with four large wings.
● See **insects** on page 57.

mother
mothers
A **mother** is a woman who has a child.

motorbike
motorbikes
A **motorbike** is a large, heavy bicycle with an engine.

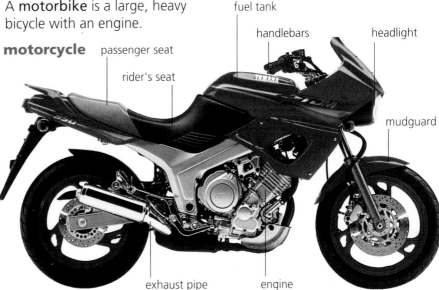

motorcycle — passenger seat
rider's seat
fuel tank
handlebars
headlight
mudguard
exhaust pipe
engine

motorway
motorways
A **motorway** is a wide road where vehicles travel fast. People drive long distances on motorways.

mountain
mountains
A **mountain** is a very high piece of land. Mountains are higher than hills.

mouse
mice
1 A **mouse** is a small, furry animal with a long tail and sharp teeth. *The **mice** chased each other through the corn.*
2 A **mouse** is also something that you use to move things on a computer screen.

mouth
mouths
Your **mouth** is the part of your face that you use to eat and talk.

move
moves moving moved
1 When things **move**, they change position and do not stay still. *The leaves **moved** in the breeze.*
2 When people **move**, they go from one place to another. *Andrew **moved** to a more comfortable chair.*
3 Move also means to stop living in one house and start living in another. *Amy **moved** to Wales.*

A B C D E F G H I J K L **M** N O P Q R S T U V W X Y Z

much

Much means a large amount.
Fran doesn't eat **much**.

mud

Mud is earth that is wet and sticky.

mug
mugs
A **mug** is a large cup with straight sides.

multiply

multiplies multiplying multiplied

When you **multiply** numbers, you add the same number to itself several times.

4 × 3 = 12

mum
mums
Mum is a name for your mother.

muscle
muscles
A **muscle** is a part of your body. Muscles are fixed to bones and pull on them to make them move.

museum
museums
A **museum** is a place where you can see interesting things.

mushroom
mushrooms
A **mushroom** is a plant that looks like an umbrella. You can eat some mushrooms.

music
Music is a pattern of sounds. People make music by playing musical instruments or by singing.

musical instrument
musical instruments
A **musical instrument** is something that you use to make music. You can play musical instruments by blowing into them or hitting them, or by pulling their strings.

must
If you **must** do something, you have to do it. *I* **must** *go now.*

mustn't
Mustn't is a short way of saying must not. *You* **mustn't** *go home yet.*

musical instruments

violin and bow

guitar

cello

flute

harmonica

clarinet

trumpet

saxophone

myself

Myself means me and nobody else. *I have hurt* **myself**.

mysterious

Something that is **mysterious** is difficult to understand or explain. *We heard a* **mysterious** *sound.*

bongos

triangle

cymbals

chime bars

tambourine

maracas

Nn

nag

nags nagging nagged

If someone **nags** you, they keep telling you to do something. *Mum keeps* **nagging** *me to do up my laces.*

nail

nails

1 A **nail** is a piece of metal with a point at one end. You use nails to join pieces of wood together.
2 Your **nails** are the hard parts at the ends of your fingers and toes.

naked

Someone who is **naked** is not wearing any clothes.

name

names

A **name** is what you call a person or a thing. *My friend's* **name** *is Tim.*

nap

naps

If you have a **nap**, you sleep for a short time.

napkin

napkins

A **napkin** is a piece of cloth or paper that you use to protect your clothes when you eat.

nappy

nappies

A **nappy** is a pad of cloth or tissue that covers a baby's bottom.

narrow

narrower narrowest

If something is **narrow**, its sides are not far apart. *We rode down the* **narrow** *path.*

■ *opposite* **wide**

nasty

nastier nastiest

Someone who is **nasty** is cruel and unkind. *A* **nasty** *witch.*

natural

Something that is **natural** has not been made by people or machines. *Wood is a* **natural** *material.*

nature

Nature is everything in the world that has not been made by people. Plants, animals and the weather are all parts of nature.

naughty

naughtier naughtiest

Someone who is **naughty** behaves badly. *Sophie was very* **naughty** *today. She threw her lunch out of the window.*

near

nearer nearest

If something is **near**, it is only a short distance away. *The park is very* **near** *our house.*

■ *opposite* **far**

nearly

Nearly means almost, but not quite. *Ruth is* **nearly** *140 centimetres high. I* **nearly** *won the race today.*

A B C D E F G H I J K L M N O P Q R S T U V W X Y Z

neat
neater neatest
Something that is **neat** is very tidy.
*Please make your handwriting
neat so that I can read it. Carly
has tidied her bedroom so that it
looks really neat.*

neck
necks
Your **neck** is the part of your body
that joins your head to your
shoulders.

necklace
necklaces
A **necklace** is a string of beads
or a chain that you wear round
your neck.
● *See* **jewellery** *on page 59.*

Some words that begin
with an "n" sound, such as
knee, knife, knock and **know,**
are spelt "kn".

need
needs needing needed
If you **need** something, you must
have it. *Human beings need food
and water to live.*

needle
needles
1 A **needle**
is a very thin,
pointed piece of metal that you
use for sewing. You put thread
through a hole in the needle.
2 Knitting **needles** are long sticks
made of plastic or metal. People
use knitting needles to knit clothes
out of wool.

needn't
Needn't is a short way of saying
need not. *You needn't rush,
there's plenty of time.*

neighbour
neighbours
A **neighbour** is someone who
lives near you.

neither
Neither means not one or the
other. *Neither of the two boys
knew the way home.*

nephew
nephews
Someone's **nephew** is the son of
their sister or their brother.

nervous
1 If you are **nervous** about
something, you are worried or
excited about it. *Tom is nervous
about his first trip in a plane.*
2 A **nervous** person or animal is
easily frightened. *Don't scare the
kittens. They're very nervous.*

nest
nests
A **nest** is a home made by birds
and some animals. Birds keep their
eggs and their babies in a nest.

net
nets
1 A **net** is a bag made of knotted
thread or rope. Nets are used to
catch fish. *Jon caught some fish in
his net and then put them back in
the water.*
2 When you play tennis, you hit
the ball over a **net**. Tennis nets are
made of knotted rope.

never
Never means not at any time. *You
must never talk to strangers.*
■ *opposite* **always**

new
newer newest
1 If something is **new**, it has just
been made. *A new bicycle.*
■ *opposite* **old**
2 **New** can also mean different.
There is a new family next door.

news
1 **News** is information about
things that are happening in the
world. *Dad always listens to the
news on the radio.*
2 **News** is also information about
things that have happened to you.
*I've had some good news. I'm in
the school team.*

newspaper
newspapers
A **newspaper** is made of several
sheets of paper with stories and
pictures about the news. Most
newspapers come out every day.

newt
newts
A **newt** is
a small
creature
with short
legs and
a long
tail. Newts
live on
land and
lay their
eggs in water.

next
1 **Next** means the one after this.
*We're all going on holiday
next week.*
2 **Next** also means nearest. *Jason
sits next to me at school.*

nice
nicer nicest
If you think that something is **nice**, you like it. *A nice meal. A nice day.*

> **Some other words for**
> **nice** are **beautiful**, **pleasant**, **good**, **lovely** and **enjoyable**.

nickname
nicknames
A **nickname** is a name that you give to a friend. *Jim's nickname is Carrots because he has red hair.*

niece
nieces
Someone's **niece** is the daughter of their sister or their brother.

night
Night is the time when it is dark outside. People sleep at night.

nightie
nighties
A **nightie** is a loose dress that girls and women wear in bed.

nightmare
nightmares
A **nightmare** is a horrible, frightening dream.

nobody
Nobody means no person. *There was nobody in the house.*

nod
nods nodding nodded
When you **nod**, you move your head up and down. People often nod to show that they agree.

noise
noises
A **noise** is a sound. *We heard a noise coming from the cellar.*

noisy
noisier noisiest
If something is **noisy**, it is very loud. *I wish that Rupert's drums were not quite so noisy.*

none
None means not one or not any. *Jonathan went to buy some doughnuts, but there were none left.*

nonsense
Something that is **nonsense** is silly and does not mean anything. *Katy is talking nonsense again.*

noon
Noon is 12 o'clock in the middle of the day.

no one
No one means no person. *There was no one in when I got home.*

normal
Something that is **normal** is ordinary and usual. *I got up at the normal time.*

north
North is a direction. If you look at the Sun when it rises, north is on your left.

nose
noses
Your **nose** is the part of your face that you use to smell and breathe.

note
notes
1 A **note** is a sound that you make when you sing or play a musical instrument. A piece of music is made up of many different notes.
2 A **note** is also a short message that you write down.
3 A **note** is also a piece of paper money. *A £5 note.*

nothing
Nothing means not a thing. *There was nothing left in Pepper's bowl.*

notice
notices noticing noticed
If you **notice** something, you see it and pay attention to it. *Becky noticed that Eric looked pale.*

now
Now means at this time. *It's raining now, so let's go out later.*

number
numbers
A **number** is a word or a sign that shows you how many there are. Four and thirty-three are numbers. 9 and 27 are also numbers.

nurse
nurses
A **nurse** is someone who looks after people who are ill or hurt. Nurses often work in hospitals.

nursery
nurseries
1 A **nursery** is a place where young children are looked after while their parents are at work.
2 A **nursery** is also a place where you can buy plants.

nut
nuts
A **nut** has a hard shell and usually grows on a tree. Many nuts can be eaten.

Oo

oar
oars

An **oar** is a long pole with a wide end. You use oars to row a boat.

obey
obeys obeying obeyed

When you **obey** someone, you do what they tell you to do. *Garth is teaching his puppy to obey him.*

■ *opposite* **disobey**

object
objects

An **object** is a thing that you can touch and see. Objects are not alive. Computers, toys, books and furniture are all objects.

obvious

If something is **obvious**, it is easy to see or easy to understand.

ocean
oceans

An **ocean** is a very large sea. There are five oceans in the world.

o'clock

You use the word **o'clock** when you say what time it is. O'clock is short for of the clock. *It is now seven o'clock.*

octopus
octopuses

An **octopus** is a sea creature with a soft body and eight long arms.

odd
odder oddest

1 An **odd** number cannot be divided exactly by two.
1, 3, 5 and 7 are odd numbers.
■ *opposite* **even**
2 If something is **odd**, it is strange or unusual. *An odd hat.*
3 **Odd** things are not part of a pair or a set. *Odd socks.*

off

1 When you turn **off** a machine, you make it stop working.
■ *opposite* **on**
2 **Off** also means away from something. *Take the plates off the table.*
■ *opposite* **on**

offer
offers offering offered

1 If you **offer** to do something, you say that you will do it. *Adam offered to make the tea.*
2 If you **offer** someone something, you ask them if they would like it. *Tessa offered a sandwich to her aunt.*

office
offices

An **office** is a room or a building where people work at desks.

often

If you do something **often**, you do it a lot. *We often go skating.*

oil
oils

Oil is a thick liquid. Some oil comes from the ground and is used to work machines and to make heat. Some oil comes from plants and is used for cooking.

old
older oldest

1 Someone who is **old** has lived for a long time. *An old man.*
■ *opposite* **young**
2 Something that is **old** has been used for a long time. *Old clothes.*
■ *opposite* **new**

on

1 When you turn **on** a machine, you make it start working.
■ *opposite* **off**
2 **On** also means touching the surface of something. *Put the plates on the table.*
■ *opposite* **off**
3 **On** also means about. *Louise bought a book on cats.*
4 You use **on** to say when something happened. *We went out for lunch on Friday.*

once

1 If something happens **once**, it happens one time. *I've only been to London* **once**.
2 **Once** also means after. ***Once*** *we've had lunch, we can go out.*

onion

onions
An **onion** is a round vegetable with a strong taste and smell. Onions grow under the ground.

only

Only means just one and not any others. *There's* **only** *one cake left.*

open

opens opening opened
1 If you **open** a door, you move it so that you can go through it.
◼ *opposite* **close**
2 If you **open** a box, you take its lid off, so that you can put things in or take things out of it.
◼ *opposite* **close**

open

If something is **open**, people can go through it or into it. *The door is* **open**. *The shop is* **open** *all day.*

operation

operations
When someone has an **operation**, part of their body is repaired, replaced or removed.

opposite

opposites
The **opposite** of something is the thing that is most different from it. *The* **opposite** *of dark is light.*

opposite

If two people are **opposite** one another, they face each other. *My friend sat* **opposite** *me, on the other side of the table.*

orange

oranges
1 **Orange** is the colour that you make when you mix red and yellow. Carrots are orange.
2 An **orange** is a round, juicy fruit with a thick, orange skin.

orchard

orchards
An **orchard** is a piece of land where fruit trees are grown.

orchestra

orchestras
An **orchestra** is a large group of people who play different musical instruments together. *The* **orchestra** *gave a concert.*

order

Order is the way that things are arranged. *Liza arranged her dolls in* **order** *of size, from the smallest to the biggest.*

order

orders ordering ordered
1 If someone **orders** you to do something, they tell you to do it.
2 If you **order** food in a restaurant, you say that you want it.

ordinary

If something is **ordinary**, it is usual and not special. *It was just an* **ordinary** *day.*

organ

organs
1 An **organ** is a musical instrument with keys like a piano and lots of pipes of different sizes. When you press the keys, air is pushed through the pipes to make notes.
2 An **organ** is also a part of your body that does a particular job. Your heart and lungs are organs.

organize

organizes organizing organized
When you **organize** something, you plan it so that it happens in the way that you want it to. *We are* **organizing** *a party.*

ornament

ornaments
An **ornament** is a small object that you put in a room because it looks good. *Amanda arranged the* **ornaments** *on a shelf.*

ostrich

ostriches

An **ostrich** is a large bird with a long neck and long legs. Ostriches can run very fast, but they cannot fly.

other

1 **Other** means something different. *Do you have any other games?*
2 **Other** also means one of two things. *I can't find my other shoe.*

otter

otters

An **otter** is an animal with brown fur and a long tail. Otters live near water and they catch fish to eat.

ought

If you **ought** to do something, you should do it. *You ought to practise the piano.*

out

Out means not inside. *We went out for some fresh air. We took the books out of the box.*

■ *opposite* **in**

outdoors

If you are **outdoors**, you are not in a building. *In the summer, we play outdoors.*

■ *opposite* **indoors**

outing

outings

If you go on an **outing**, you visit somewhere, usually for a day. *Our class had an outing to a castle.*

outline

outlines

An **outline** is a line around the edge of something. *Rosa drew an outline of the leaf.*

outside

1 If something is **outside** a thing, it is not in it. *I left my shoes outside my bedroom.*
2 **Outside** also means outdoors. *We went outside as soon as it stopped raining.*

oval

ovals

An **oval** is a shape like an egg.

● See **shapes** on page 106.

oven

ovens

An **oven** is the part of a cooker that you use for baking or roasting food.

over

1 **Over** means on top of something. *Tim wore a jumper over his shirt.*

■ *opposite* **under**
2 **Over** also means above or across something. *A plane flew over the house. Ed jumped over the pond.*
3 If something is **over**, it is finished. *When the party was over, we went home.*
4 **Over** also means down. *John fell over. Kate knocked over the vase.*

overboard

If someone falls **overboard**, they fall off a boat, into the water.

overtake

overtakes overtaking overtook overtaken

When one vehicle **overtakes** another, it goes past it. *Dad overtook a lorry on the motorway.*

owe

owes owing owed

If you **owe** someone money, you have to pay them what you have borrowed.

owl

owls

An **owl** is a bird with large eyes. Owls hunt at night.

own

owns owning owned

If you **own** something, it belongs to you. *Richard owns two goldfish and three mice.*

ox

oxen

An **ox** is a large animal with horns. Oxen are often used to carry or pull things.

Pp

pack
packs packing packed
When you **pack** a bag or a suitcase, you put things in it.

package
packages
A **package** is a small parcel.

packet
packets
A **packet** is a small container made from paper, card or plastic. *A packet of seeds.*

pad
pads
1 A **pad** has many pages joined together at one side. You can write or draw on a pad.
2 A **pad** is also a thick piece of soft material.

paddle
paddles paddling paddled
When you **paddle**, you walk in shallow water. *Lucy and Pete paddled in the sea.*

padlock
padlocks
A **padlock** is a kind of lock. You fasten things together with a padlock to keep them safe. *We use a padlock to lock the shed.*

page
pages
A **page** is a piece of paper in a book or a pad.

paid
Paid comes from the word **pay**. *You must pay for your ticket before the show starts. We have already paid for ours.*

pain
Pain is what you feel when you are hurt or ill.

painful
If something is **painful**, it hurts a lot. *A painful knee.*

paint
paints
Paint is a liquid that you use to put colour on things.

paint
paints painting painted
1 When you **paint**, you use a brush and paints to make a picture.
2 If you **paint** a room, you put paint on its walls.

pair
pairs
A **pair** is the name for two things that go together. *A pair of socks.*

palace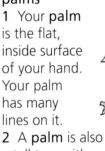
palaces
A **palace** is a large house where kings, queens or other very important people live.

pale
paler palest
Pale colours have a lot of white in them. *Melanie painted her room pale blue.*

palm
palms
1 Your **palm** is the flat, inside surface of your hand. Your palm has many lines on it.
2 A **palm** is also a tall tree with large leaves at the top of its trunk. Palms grow in hot countries.

pancake
pancakes
A **pancake** is a kind of thin, flat cake. You make pancakes by frying a mixture of milk, eggs and flour.

panda
pandas
A **panda** is a black and white bear. Pandas live in China.

A B C D E F G H I J K L M N O **P** Q R S T U V W X Y Z

panic
panics panicking panicked
If you **panic**, you have a sudden feeling of fear. *Louise panicked when she couldn't find her mum.*

pant
pants panting panted
When you **pant**, you breathe quickly and loudly because you are out of breath. *Raymond was panting after his run.*

panther
panthers
A **panther** is a leopard, usually a black one.

pantomime
pantomimes
A **pantomime** is a play with songs and jokes. A pantomime tells the story of a fairy tale. *We went to see the pantomime "Aladdin".*

pants
Pants is the name for the underwear that covers your bottom.

paper
papers
1 **Paper** is the material that is used for writing, making books and wrapping things.
2 **Paper** is short for **newspaper**.

parachute
parachutes
A **parachute** is a large piece of cloth with strings attached to it. Parachutes are used to drop people or things safely to the ground from a plane.

parcel
parcels
A **parcel** is something wrapped in paper. Parcels are usually sent through the post.

parent
parents
A **parent** is a mother or a father.

park
parks
A **park** is a large piece of land where people can walk or play.

park
parks parking parked
When someone **parks** their car, they leave it on the street or in a car park.

parrot
parrots
A **parrot** is a brightly coloured bird with a curved beak. Some parrots can talk.

part
parts
A **part** of a thing belongs to that thing. *Wheels and pedals are parts of a bicycle.*

particular
Particular means this one and not any others. *This particular book is very helpful.*

partner
partners
A **partner** is someone you do something with. *Peter is my dancing partner.*

party
parties
If you have a **party**, you invite your friends to eat and have fun with you. *A birthday party.*

pass
passes passing passed
1 If you **pass** someone or something, you go past them. *We passed you as we drove home.*
2 If you **pass** something to someone, you give it to them. *Pass me your plate please.*
3 If you **pass** a test, you do well in it.

passage
passages
A **passage** is a narrow path, usually between two buildings.

passenger
passengers
A **passenger** is someone who travels in a vehicle and is not the driver.

past

The **past** is the period of time that has already happened. *This story is set in the* **past** *when no one had televisions or telephones.*

past

Past also means by or beside. *The main road goes* **past** *our house.*

paste

Paste is a soft, sticky mixture that you can spread. *Wallpaper* **paste**.

pastry

Pastry is a food made from flour, butter and water. You roll it flat and use it for making pies.

pat

pats patting patted

If you **pat** something, you touch it gently with your hand. *Leo* **patted** *Fido on the back.*

patch

patches

A **patch** is a small piece of cloth that you sew on clothes to cover a hole. *Laura has a* **patch** *on her jeans.*

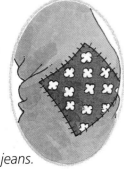

path

paths

A **path** is a narrow road for people to walk along. *This* **path** *goes through the wood.*

patient

patients

A **patient** is someone who is ill or hurt and is looked after by a doctor or a nurse.

patient

Someone who is **patient** can wait for a long time without getting annoyed.

pattern

patterns

A **pattern** is the way that lines, shapes and colours are arranged. *I like the* **pattern** *on your curtains.*

pause

pauses pausing paused

When you **pause**, you stop what you are doing for a short time.

pavement

pavements

A **pavement** is a hard path beside a road. You walk on the pavement.

paw

paws

A **paw** is an animal's foot. Dogs and cats have paws.

pay

pays paying paid

If you **pay** someone, you give them money for something.

pea

peas

A **pea** is a small, round, green vegetable. Peas grow in pods.

peaceful

When it is **peaceful**, it is quiet.

peach

peaches

A **peach** is a round, soft fruit with a furry skin. A peach has a stone in the middle of it.

peacock

peacocks

A **peacock** is a large bird with long, colourful tail feathers.

peak

peaks

1 The **peak** of a mountain is the point at its top.
2 The **peak** of a cap is the part at the front that sticks out.

— peak

peanut

peanuts

A **peanut** is a small, oval nut. Peanuts have shells and grow under the ground.

pear
pears
A **pear** is a juicy fruit. Pears are rounded at the bottom and get narrower towards the top.

pebble
pebbles
A **pebble** is a smooth, round stone. You find pebbles on beaches.

peculiar
If something is **peculiar**, it is unusual or strange. *Aunt Dottie has a peculiar habit of talking to flowers.*

pedal
pedals
A **pedal** is a part of a bicycle. You press the pedals with your feet to make the bicycle move.

peel
The **peel** on a fruit or a vegetable is its skin. *Orange peel.*

peep
peeps peeping peeped
If you **peep** at something, you have a quick look at it. *Sophie peeped at the sleeping baby.*

peg
pegs
1 A **peg** is a hook that you use to hang things on.
2 You also use **pegs** to hold clothes on a washing line. Pegs are made from wood or plastic.

pen
pens
You use a **pen** to write or draw in ink. Pens are made from plastic or metal.

pencil
pencils
A **pencil** is a long, thin piece of wood with a black stick in the middle of it, called a lead. You use a pencil to write or draw.

penguin
penguins
A **penguin** is a black and white bird that lives in very cold places. Penguins cannot fly. They use their wings to swim.

penny
pence *or* pennies
A **penny** is a coin. In Britain, there are 100 pennies in a pound.

people
People are men, women and children.

pepper
You shake **pepper** over your food to give it flavour. Pepper tastes hot.

perch
perches perching perched
Perch means to sit or stand on the edge of something. *The bird perched on the branch.*

perfect
If something is **perfect**, it is exactly right. *Victoria practised the tune on her recorder until it was perfect.*

performance
performances
A **performance** is something that you do in front of lots of people, such as singing, acting or playing an instrument.

perfume
perfumes
Perfume is a liquid that smells nice. People put perfume on their skin.

perhaps
You say **perhaps** when you mean that something is possible, but not certain. *Perhaps we'll see you this weekend.*

period
periods
A **period** is a length of time. *Robert left the room for a short period.*

permission
If you have **permission** to do something, you are allowed to do it. *Lisa was given permission to leave school early.*

person
A **person** is a man, a woman or a child.

persuade
persuades persuading
persuaded
If you **persuade** someone to do something, you make them agree to do it. *Allie **persuaded** me to wait for her.*

pest
pests
A **pest** is a person or an animal that makes trouble.

pet
pets
A **pet** is an animal that lives with you at home. Cats and dogs are pets. *Jo keeps guinea pigs as **pets**.*

petal
petals
A **petal** is the white or coloured part of a flower. *The roses had pink **petals**.*

petrol
Petrol is a liquid that you put in a vehicle to make it go.

phone
phones
Phone is short for telephone.

photograph
photographs
A **photograph** is a picture that you take with a camera.

piano
pianos
A **piano** is a large musical instrument with a row of black and white keys. You press the keys with your fingers to play different notes.

pick
picks picking picked
1 If you **pick** up something, you lift it up. *Kim **picked** up the kitten.*
2 When you **pick** something, you choose it. *Pick any cake you want.*
3 If you **pick** fruit or flowers, you take them from a plant or a tree.

picnic
picnics
A **picnic** is a meal that you take with you to eat outdoors.

picture
pictures
A **picture** is a painting, a drawing or a photograph.

pie
pies
A **pie** is a pastry case filled with meat, vegetables or fruit. Pies are baked in an oven.

piece
pieces
A **piece** of something is a part of it. *A **piece** of the jigsaw is missing.*

pier
piers
A **pier** is a long platform that is built out over the sea. Piers often have games and rides on them.

pig
pigs
A **pig** is an animal with a fat body, short legs and a curly tail.

pigeon
pigeons
A **pigeon** is a grey bird with a fat body and a small head.
▲ *say pij-in*

pile
piles
A **pile** is a lot of things that have been put on top of each other. *A **pile** of clothes.*

pill
pills

A **pill** is a small, dry piece of medicine. People swallow pills when they are ill to make them well again.

pillow
pillows

A **pillow** is a soft pad that you rest your head on, when you are lying in bed.

pilot
pilots

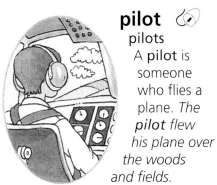

A **pilot** is someone who flies a plane. *The pilot flew his plane over the woods and fields.*

pin
pins

A **pin** is a small, thin piece of metal with a point at one end. You use pins to hold pieces of cloth together.

pinch
pinches pinching pinched

If you **pinch** someone, you squeeze their skin between your thumb and finger.

pineapple
pineapples

A **pineapple** is a large, oval fruit with a tough skin and pointed leaves at the top.

pink
Pink is the colour that you make when you mix red and white. Strawberry ice cream is pink.

pipe
pipes

A **pipe** is a long tube that carries gas or liquids.

pirate
pirates

A **pirate** is someone who attacks ships at sea and steals things from them.

pit
pits

A **pit** is a deep hole in the ground.

pitch
pitches

A **pitch** is an area of ground where people play games, such as football.

pity
pities pitying pitied

If you **pity** someone, you feel sorry for them.

pizza
pizzas

A **pizza** is a flat piece of special bread with tomatoes and cheese on top. You can also have vegetables, meat or fish on pizzas. Pizzas are usually round and are baked in an oven.

place
places

A **place** is somewhere. Places can be very big, like a country, or very small. *Africa is a very hot place. Can you find a place to put your mug?*

place
places placing placed

If you **place** a thing somewhere, you put it there. *Place the vase in the middle of the table.*

plain
plainer plainest

1 Something that is **plain** is ordinary and not decorated. *Gary prefers plain food. I have plain curtains in my room.*
2 If something is **plain**, it is clear and easy to understand. *Ben made it plain that he did not like peas.*

plan
plans

A **plan** is a map of a building or a place. *Katy drew a plan of her bedroom.*

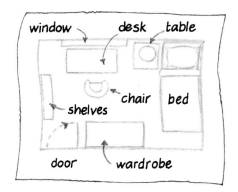

plan
plans planning planned

If you **plan** something, you decide how you will do it. *We planned the treasure hunt carefully.*

plane
planes

Plane is short for **aeroplane**.

planet

planets

A **planet** is a huge, round object that moves round the Sun. The Earth is a planet.

planets

Pluto

Neptune

Uranus

Saturn

Jupiter

Mars   Earth   Venus   Mercury

Sun

plank

planks

A **plank** is a long, flat piece of wood.

plant

plants

A **plant** is a living thing that grows in soil or in water. Trees, flowers and seaweed are plants.

plaster

plasters

1 A **plaster** is a sticky strip with a soft pad in the middle, that you use to protect a cut.
2 A **plaster** is also a hard case that holds the parts of a broken bone together until they are mended.

plastic

Plastic is a light material that does not break easily. Plastic is used to make bottles, buckets and many other things.

plate

plates

A **plate** is a flat dish that you put food on.

platform

platforms

1 A **platform** is a raised area in a room.
2 A **platform** is also the place where you stand to wait for a train.

play

plays

A **play** is a story that you act.

play

plays playing played

1 When you **play**, you do something for fun. *The boys are playing in the park.*
2 If you **play** a sport, you take part in it. *Mickey is playing football.*
3 If you **play** a musical instrument, you use it to make music. *Charlotte is playing her recorder.*

playground

playgrounds

A **playground** is a place where you can play outdoors. Playgrounds often have swings and other play equipment.

pleasant

If something is **pleasant**, you enjoy it. *We had a pleasant walk.*

please

pleases pleasing pleased

If you **please** someone, you make them happy. *Carlo pleased his mother by tidying his room.*

please

You say **please** when you ask for something in a polite way. *Please may I have an apple?*

plenty

If there is **plenty** of something, there is a lot of it. *We have plenty of food for our picnic.*

plough

ploughs

A **plough** is a set of sharp blades that are pulled by a tractor. Ploughs are used to dig up earth in fields.

pluck
plucks plucking plucked
When you **pluck** the strings of a guitar, you pull on them with your fingers to make notes.

plug
plugs
1 A **plug** is a round piece of plastic or rubber. You use a plug to keep water in a sink or a bath.
2 A **plug** is also a small object that connects a machine to the electric power.

plum
plums
A **plum** is a soft fruit with yellow, red or purple skin. A plum has a stone in the middle of it.

plump
plumper plumpest
Someone who is **plump** is rather fat. *A **plump** baby.*

plus
Plus means add. The sign for plus is +. *Three **plus** four equals seven.*

pocket
pockets
A **pocket** is a small bag that is sewn on to clothes. You can keep things in your pockets.

pocket money
Pocket money is money that your parents give you to spend.

pod
pods
A **pod** is a part of a plant that contains seeds. Peas and beans grow in pods.

poem
poems
A **poem** is a piece of writing. Poems usually have short lines and often have words that rhyme.

The Hungry Dragon

"I like you, knight," the dragon said,
"You're sweet enough to eat.
I'd like you best spread on my bread
with sliced tomatoes at your head
and lettuce by your feet."

The knight let out a frightened squeal,
"Don't eat me, please!" he said,
"I'd be impossible to peel
and wouldn't make a tasty meal.
Try sausages instead!"

point
points
1 A **point** is the sharp end of something. *A pencil **point**.*
2 A **point** is also part of a score in a game or a competition. *Our team won seven **points**.*

point
points pointing pointed
If you **point** at something, you use your finger to show where it is. *Karma **pointed** at the squirrels in the bushes.*

poisonous
If you eat something **poisonous**, it can make you very ill or even kill you. Some berries are poisonous.

polar bear
polar bears
A **polar bear** is a large, white bear that lives near the North Pole.

pole
poles
A **pole** is a long piece of wood or metal. *A flag **pole**.*

police
The **police** protect people and make sure that the law is obeyed.

polish
polishes polishing polished
When you **polish** something, you rub it to make it clean and shiny. *Justin **polished** his dad's car.*

For Internet links, go to
www.usborne-quicklinks.com
89
*po*lite *to* *po*stcard

polite
politer politest
A **polite** person has good manners and thinks about other people's feelings.
■ *opposite* **rude**

pollution
Pollution is damage to the environment. Traffic fumes and litter are types of pollution.

pond
ponds
A **pond** is a small area of water.

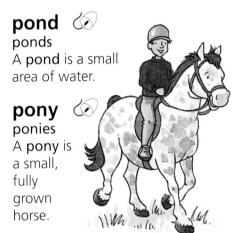

pony
ponies
A **pony** is a small, fully grown horse.

pool
pools
1 A **pool** is a small area of water.
2 A **pool** is also a place where people swim. *A public pool.*

poor
poorer poorest
1 People who are **poor** do not have much money.
■ *opposite* **rich**
2 If something is **poor**, it is not very good. *Poor handwriting.*

pop
pops popping popped
If something **pops**, it explodes with a small bang. *The balloon popped when the cat jumped on it.*

poppy
poppies
A **poppy** is a flower with large petals. Poppies are usually red.

popular
Someone who is **popular** is liked by many people. *Jodie is very popular. She has lots of friends.*

porridge
Porridge is oatmeal cooked in milk or water.

port
ports
A **port** is a town with a harbour.

position
positions
1 The **position** of something is the place where it is. *Sarah's house is in a wonderful position, just next to the park.*
2 Someone's **position** is the way that they are standing or sitting.

possession
possessions
A **possession** is something that you own. *Don't leave any of your possessions on the coach.*

possible
If something is **possible**, it can happen or it can be done. *Is it possible to catch a bus into town?*

post
posts
A **post** is a long, thick piece of wood, metal or concrete that is fixed in the ground.

post
posts posting posted
If you **post** a letter, you put it in a letter box to be sent to someone.

postcard
postcards
A **postcard** is a card that you post without an envelope. Postcards usually have a picture on one side.

POSTCARD

Dear Simon
You wouldn't believe how hot it is here! The sea is amazingly clear and blue and we've been swimming every day. I've collected lots of shells and seen some really strange creatures in the rock pools.
See you soon.
Lucy

Simon Small
12 Hilltop Road
CASTLETOWN
Wessex
UK

A B C D E F G H I J K L M N O **P** Q R S T U V W X Y Z

poster
posters
A **poster** is a large picture or notice that is stuck on a wall. *Kevin has covered his bedroom wall with posters.*

post office
post offices
A **post office** is a place where you can buy stamps and post letters and parcels.

pot
pots
1 A **pot** is a deep, round container. People use pots for cooking food.
2 A **pot** is also a container for a plant.

potato
potatoes
A **potato** is a rounded vegetable that grows under the ground.

pottery
Pottery is a name for objects, such as bowls and mugs, that are made out of clay.

pound
pounds
A **pound** is a unit of money. In Britain, a pound is made up of 100 pennies. The sign for a pound is £.

pour
pours pouring poured
When you **pour** a liquid, you tip it out of its container.

powder
powders
Powder is made up of lots of very tiny grains. Flour is a powder.

power
1 If someone has **power**, they control other people or things.
2 **Power** is also the strength or energy that something has. *Dad wants to buy a car with more power.*
3 **Power** is another name for electricity. *Our power was cut off in the storm.*

practise
practises practising practised
If you **practise** something, you do it again and again so that you get better at it. *Abby practises playing the trumpet every day.*

precious
1 A **precious** object is worth a lot of money. *Princess Aurora has a chest of precious jewels.*

2 Something that is **precious** is very important or special to you.
▲ *say presh-us*

prefer
prefers preferring preferred
If you **prefer** something, you like it better than another thing. *I prefer apples to oranges.*

prepare
prepares preparing prepared
If you **prepare**, you get ready. *Lydia is preparing for her holiday. Guy is preparing lunch.*

present
presents
1 A **present** is something special that you give to someone.
2 The **present** is the time now. *The story begins in the present.*

president
presidents
A **president** is someone who rules a country.

press
presses pressing pressed
If you **press** something, you push it. *Press this button to turn on the television.*

pretend
pretends pretending pretended
When you **pretend**, you act as if something were true, even though it is not. *Sam pretended that he was asleep. Nicky pretended to be a frog.*

pretty
prettier prettiest
Something that is **pretty** is nice to look at.

prevent
prevents preventing prevented
If you **prevent** something, you stop it happening. *Joanna acted quickly to prevent an accident.*

prey
Prey is a name for the creatures that birds and animals hunt and eat. *The tiger chased after its prey.*

price
prices
The **price** of something is how much money it costs. *What's the price of this hat?*

prick
pricks pricking pricked
If you **prick** yourself, something sharp makes a tiny hole in your skin. *Coral has pricked her finger.*

prince
princes
A **prince** is the son of a king or a queen.

princess
princesses
A **princess** is the daughter of a king or a queen. The wife of a prince is also called a princess.

print
prints printing printed
1 When someone **prints** something, they use a machine to put words on to paper. *Mrs Parsnip printed my story for me.*
2 When you **print**, you write with letters that are not joined up.

prison
prisons
A **prison** is a place where people are kept as a punishment, because they have not obeyed the law.

private
If something is **private**, it belongs to one person only. *A private letter.*

prize
prizes
You win a **prize** as a reward for doing something well. *Carl won a cup as his prize for coming first in the race.*

probably
If something will **probably** happen, it is almost certain to happen. *It will probably rain again tomorrow.*

problem
problems
A **problem** is something difficult that you need to find an answer to. *We have a problem with our kitten. She keeps running away.*

produce
produces producing produced
1 When you **produce** something, you make it. *Mum produced a delicious lunch.*
2 If you **produce** something, you get it out so that people can see it. *Ginger produced a mouse from his pocket.*

program
programs
A **program** is a set of instructions that tells a computer how to work.

programme
programmes
1 A **programme** is something that you watch on television or hear on the radio. *A nature programme.*
2 A **programme** is also a small book or list that tells you about a play or a concert.

progress
When you make **progress**, you get better or move forwards. *Lucy is making good progress at school. The explorers made slow progress through the jungle.*

project
projects
When you do a **project**, you find out about a subject. *Our class is doing a project on sound.*

promise
promises promising promised
When you **promise**, you say that you will really do something. *Cassie promised to be on time.*

proper
Proper means right or correct. *Is this the proper way to get on a horse?*

protect
protects protecting protected
When you **protect** someone or something, you keep them safe. *Jo protected her puppy from the rain.*

proud
prouder proudest
If you feel **proud**, you are pleased about what you have done. *Josie is **proud** of her cake.*

provide
provides providing provided
When you **provide** something, you give people what they need. *The hotel **provides** lunch.*

public
If something is **public**, everyone can use it. *A **public** park.*

pudding
puddings
A **pudding** is a sweet food that you eat at the end of a meal.

puddle
puddles
A **puddle** is a small pool of water. You see puddles on the ground when it has been raining.

pull
pulls pulling pulled
If you **pull** something, you move it towards you. *Richard **pulled** his suitcase out of the cupboard.*

pump
pumps
You use a **pump** to push air or liquid into something. *A bicycle **pump**.*

punch
punches punching punched
If you **punch** something, you hit it with your fist.

punish
punishes punishing punished
If someone **punishes** you, they do something to you because you have been naughty. *Mum **punished** me for being rude by sending me to bed.*

pupil
pupils
A **pupil** is someone who learns something, usually in a school. *There are 30 **pupils** in my class.*

puppet
puppets
A **puppet** is a doll that can be made to move. Some puppets are like gloves and you move them with your fingers. Other puppets have strings that you can pull.

puppy
puppies
A **puppy** is a young dog.

purple
Purple is the colour that you make when you mix red and blue.

purpose
If you do something on **purpose**, you mean to do it. *Matt kicked his sister on **purpose** to see if she would cry.*

purr
purrs purring purred
When a cat **purrs**, it makes a low sound in its throat, to show that it is happy.

purse
purses
A **purse** is a small bag that you keep your money in.

push
pushes pushing pushed
If you **push** something, you move it in front of you or away from you. *Daniel **pushed** his bike up the hill.*

put
puts putting put
When you **put** a thing somewhere, you move it to that place. *Please **put** the milk in the fridge.*

---

puzzle
puzzles
A **puzzle** is a game that you have to think about carefully.

How do you get from cold to warm?

Move from cold to warm in three words, by answering the clues and filling in the boxes. For each answer, change just one letter from the word above.

CLUES

1 A type of string.

2 A group of letters.

3 A creature that lives in the ground.

puzzle

puzzles puzzling puzzled

If something **puzzles** you, it makes you confused. *Simon's strange message **puzzled** me.*

pyjamas

Pyjamas is the name for the matching shirt and trousers that some people wear in bed.

	C	O	L	D
1				
2				
3				
	W	A	R	M

Qq

quack

quacks quacking quacked

When a duck **quacks**, it opens its beak and makes a loud sound.

quantity

quantities

A **quantity** is an amount or a number. *A large **quantity** of sand.*

quarrel

quarrels quarrelling quarrelled

When people **quarrel**, they argue and get angry with each other. *The boys **quarrelled** over who should go first.*

quarry

quarries

A **quarry** is a place where stone is dug out of the ground.

quarter

quarters

If something is cut into **quarters**, it is cut into four pieces of the same size.

quarter

queen

queens

A **queen** is a woman who rules a country. Queens come from royal families and are not chosen by the people.

question

questions

A **question** is what you ask when you want to know something.

"What is your name?"

"Where do you live?"

"How can I help you?"

queue

queues

A **queue** is a line of people who are waiting for something. *We waited in a **queue** for the bus.* ▲ *say kyoo*

quick

quicker quickest

1 Something that is **quick** moves at a great speed.
2 If something is **quick**, it only lasts for a short time. *Miranda had a **quick** look round the house.*

quiet

quieter quietest

Someone who is **quiet** does not make much noise. ■ *opposite* **loud**

quite

1 **Quite** means rather. *It's **quite** warm outside.*
2 **Quite** also means completely. *I haven't **quite** finished my book.*

quiz

quizzes

A **quiz** is a game or a test to find out how much you know. You have to answer questions in a quiz.

Rr

rabbit
rabbits
A **rabbit** is a small, furry animal with long ears and a short tail. Rabbits live in holes under the ground.

race
races
A **race** is a competition to find out who can go fastest. *A running race.*

racket
rackets
A **racket** is a bat with strings stretched across it. You use a racket when you play tennis.

radiator
radiators
A **radiator** is used to heat a room. Radiators are made of metal and are usually filled with hot water.

radio
radios
A **radio** is a machine that receives signals through the air and sends out sounds. You can listen to music, plays and news on a radio.

raft
rafts
A **raft** is a kind of flat boat. Rafts are often made from planks of wood that are fixed together.

rag
rags
1 A **rag** is a piece of old cloth. You use rags to clean things.
2 **Rags** are also old, torn clothes. *The poor children wore **rags** and had no shoes.*

raid
raids
A **raid** is a sudden attack on an enemy. *An air **raid**.*

rail
rails
1 A **rail** is a bar that you can hold on to. *Keep holding on to the **rail** as you climb the stairs.*
2 **Rails** are long metal bars that trains and trams run on.
3 If you go somewhere by **rail**, you travel on a train.

railway
railways
A **railway** is a track for trains to travel along.

railway

rain
rains raining rained
When it **rains**, drops of water fall from the clouds.

rainbow
rainbows
A **rainbow** is a curved band of different colours that you sometimes see in the sky. Rainbows appear when the Sun shines while it is raining.

raise
raises raising raised
If you **raise** something, you lift it up. *Laura **raised** her hand to answer the question.*

rake
rakes
A **rake** is a garden tool with a long handle and metal teeth. You use a rake to collect leaves.

ran
Ran comes from the word **run**. *Kitty runs for the school team. She ran in five races last month.*

a b c d e f g h i j k l m n o p q **r** s t u v w x y z

Some words that begin with an "r" sound, such as **wrap**, are spelt "wr".

rare

rarer rarest

If something is **rare**, you do not see it very often. *A rare butterfly.*

raspberry

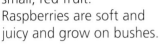

raspberries

A **raspberry** is a small, red fruit. Raspberries are soft and juicy and grow on bushes.

rat

rats

A **rat** is a small animal with a long tail and sharp teeth. Rats sometimes spread disease.

rather

1 **Rather** means a little bit. *Henrietta is rather fat.*
2 If you would **rather** do something, you want to do it more than something else. *I'd rather go to the beach than do my homework.*

raw

Food that is **raw** has not been cooked. *Raw carrots.*

reach

reaches reaching reached

1 When you **reach** for something, you stretch out your hand to touch it. *Toni jumped up to reach the ball.*
2 When you **reach** a place, you arrive there. *It was very late when we reached the hotel.*

read

reads reading read

When you **read**, you look at words and understand what they mean. *Judy is reading to her brother.*

ready

If you are **ready**, you can do something now. *I'm ready to go when you are.*

real

1 Something that is **real** is true.
2 Something that is **real** is not a copy. *A real diamond.*

really

1 **Really** means that something is true. *Men have really walked on the Moon.*
2 **Really** also means very. *Gemma was really annoyed that she had missed the bus.*

reason

reasons

If you give a **reason** for something, you explain why it has happened. *The reason I'm late is that my alarm clock didn't work.*

receive

receives receiving received

If you **receive** something, you get something that is given to you or sent to you. *I received your present in the post this morning.*

recent

Something that is **recent** happened a short time ago.

recipe

recipes

A **recipe** is a set of instructions that tell you how to make something to eat or drink.

Flapjacks

Ingredients
250g porridge oats
125g butter
60g brown sugar
10ml golden syrup
90g raisins

1 Heat the oven to 180°C/350°F/Gas Mark 4.
2 Grease a shallow tin 18 x 28cm.
3 Melt the butter, sugar and syrup in a saucepan.
4 Take the pan off the heat and add the oats and raisins. Stir together well.
5 Pour the mixture into the tin and press down. Bake for 20 minutes.
6 Cut into squares and allow to cool.

A B C D E F G H I J K L M N O P Q **R** S T U V W X Y Z

recite
recites reciting recited
When you **recite** something, such as a poem, you remember it and say it aloud.

> **Some words that begin** with an "r" sound, such as **wreck**, are spelt "wr".

recognize
recognizes recognizing recognized
If you **recognize** someone, you see them and know who they are. *I recognized Roger easily.*

record
records recording recorded
If you **record** some music or a television programme, you make a copy of it on a tape.

recorder
recorders
A **recorder** is a musical instrument. You blow into a recorder and cover the holes with your fingers to make different notes.

recover
recovers recovering recovered
When you **recover**, you get better after you have been ill.

rectangle
rectangles
A **rectangle** is a shape with four sides and four corners. It has two long sides of the same length and two short sides of the same length.

● *See* **shapes** *on page 106.*

recycle
recycles recycling recycled
If you **recycle** something, you use it again, or you use it to make something new. *Our class is collecting rubbish to recycle.*

GLASS   PAPER   METAL

red
Red is a colour. Blood and tomatoes are red.

reduce
reduces reducing reduced
If you **reduce** something, you make it smaller. *The toy shop has reduced its prices.*

referee
referees
A **referee** makes sure that the players obey the rules of a game.

reflection
reflections
You see a **reflection** when you look in a mirror or look at something shiny.

refreshments
Refreshments are food and drink. *There will be refreshments after the concert.*

refuse
refuses refusing refused
If you **refuse** to do something, you say that you will not do it.

register
registers
A **register** is a list of names. Registers are used in schools to check that everybody is there.

rehearse
rehearses rehearsing rehearsed
When you **rehearse**, you practise something before a performance. *We have been rehearsing for the concert all week.*

reindeer
reindeer
A **reindeer** is a kind of deer with large horns called antlers. Reindeer live in very cold places.

reins
Reins are the leather straps that you use to control a horse.

relative
relatives
A **relative** is a member of your family.

relax
relaxes relaxing relaxed
When you **relax**, you rest and stop worrying. *Ben relaxes by listening to music.*

remain
remains remaining remained
If you **remain** in a place, you stay there. *Clare remained at home while we went to the park.*

remember
remembers remembering remembered
When you **remember** something, you think of it again. *Simon has remembered where he left his jacket.*
■ opposite **forget**

remind
reminds reminding reminded
If you **remind** someone about something, you help them to remember it. *Julian reminded me to send a birthday card to Emily.*

remove
removes removing removed
When you **remove** something, you take it away. *I didn't recognize Sue until she removed her mask.*

rent
rents renting rented
If you **rent** a house, you pay money to its owner so that you can live in it.

repair
repairs repairing repaired
When you **repair** something, you mend it so that it can be used again.

repeat
repeats repeating repeated
If you **repeat** something, you say it again or do it again. *Please repeat your name so that I can write it down.*

replace
replaces replacing replaced
1 If you **replace** something, you put another thing in its place. *Kenny replaced the broken vase with a new one.*
2 **Replace** also means to put something back where it came from. *Shazia replaced the book on the shelf.*

reply
replies
A **reply** is an answer that you give to someone. Replies can be spoken or written down.

reply
replies replying replied
When you **reply**, you give an answer. *"No thank you,"* Peter **replied**.

reptile
reptiles
A **reptile** is an animal with dry, scaly skin. Reptiles lay eggs. Snakes, lizards and crocodiles are reptiles.

require
requires requiring required
If you **require** something, you need it. *You will require paper, scissors and glue to make this model boat.*

rescue
rescues rescuing rescued
If you **rescue** someone, you help them to escape from danger. *The helicopter crew rescued the boy from the sea.*

responsible

1 If you are **responsible** for something, you have to do it. *I am responsible for feeding Tibbles.*
2 A **responsible** person is sensible and can be trusted.

rest

The **rest** is what is left. *I ate the rest of the pizza the next day.*

rest

rests resting rested
When you **rest**, you sit down or lie down because you are tired.

restaurant

restaurants
A **restaurant** is a place with tables and chairs, where you buy and eat meals.

> **Some words that begin** with an "r" sound, such as **wrestle**, **wrist** and **write**, are spelt "wr".

result

results
A **result** is something that happens because of something else. *I got lost and as a result I was late.*

return

returns returning returned
1 If you **return** to a place, you come back to it.
2 If you **return** something, you give it back. *Ned returned the books that he had borrowed.*

reverse

reverses reversing reversed
When someone **reverses** a car, they drive it backwards.

revolting

If something is **revolting**, it makes you feel sick. *A revolting smell.*

reward

rewards
A **reward** is something that you are given because you have done something good.

rhinoceros

rhinoceroses
A **rhinoceros** is a large, heavy animal with thick, wrinkled skin. Rhinoceroses have one or two horns on their noses.

rhyme

rhymes rhyming rhymed
Words that **rhyme** end with the same sound. Fight, kite and might all rhyme.

rhythm

rhythms
A **rhythm** is a repeated pattern of sound. Music and poems have rhythm.

rib

ribs
A **rib** is one of the bones that curves round from your back to your chest. Your ribs protect your heart and your lungs.

ribbon

ribbons
A **ribbon** is a long piece of material that you tie around things. *Alice tied a ribbon round the parcel.*

rice

Rice is a food that comes from a type of grass plant. Rice grains can be cooked and eaten.

rich

richer richest
People who are **rich** have a lot of money.
■ *opposite* **poor**

riddle

riddles
A **riddle** is a question with a surprising and clever answer.

ride

rides
1 A **ride** is a journey in a vehicle or on an animal. *It's a long car ride to my uncle's house.*
2 When you have a **ride** at a fair, you go on a machine that spins you round or turns you upside down.

ride

rides riding rode ridden
If you **ride** a bicycle or a horse, you sit on it and move along.

ridiculous

Something that is **ridiculous** is very silly. *Andrew looks **ridiculous** in his mum's hat.*

right

1 Something that is **right** is correct and does not have any mistakes in it.
■ *opposite* **wrong**
2 You have a **right** hand and a left hand. Most people draw with their right hand.
■ *opposite* **left**

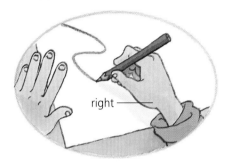

right

ring

rings

A **ring** is a band that you wear on your finger.
● *See* **jewellery** *on page 59.*

ring

rings ringing rang rung
1 When you **ring** someone, you call them on the telephone.
2 When a bell **rings**, it makes a loud noise.

rink

rinks

A **rink** is a place where you can ice-skate or roller-skate.

rinse

rinses rinsing rinsed
When you **rinse** something, you clean it in water.

rip

rips ripping ripped
If you **rip** something, you tear it. *Vincent **ripped** his trousers on the fence.*

ripe

riper ripest
If food is **ripe**, it is ready to be eaten. *A **ripe** banana.*

rise

rises rising rose risen
When something **rises**, it moves up. *The balloon **rose** into the air.*

risk

risks
If you take a **risk**, you do something that you know could be dangerous. *Robert took a **risk** when he jumped backwards into the pool.*

river

rivers
A **river** is a large amount of water running across land. Rivers have banks on either side. They run into lakes or seas.

road

roads
A **road** is a hard strip of ground that goes from one place to another. Vehicles travel on roads.

roar

roars
roaring
roared
When an animal **roars**, it makes a loud, low sound in its throat. *The lion **roared**.*

roast

roasts roasting roasted
When you **roast** food, you cook it in a hot oven. *Mum has **roasted** a chicken for lunch.*

rob

robs robbing robbed
People who **rob** take things that do not belong to them. *Three men **robbed** the bank yesterday.*

robin

robins
A **robin** is a small bird with a red chest.

robot

robots
A **robot** is a machine that can do some jobs that people do. Some robots look a bit like people.

rock

rocks
1 **Rock** is the very hard part of the Earth. Mountains are made of rock.
2 A **rock** is a large stone.

rock

rocks rocking rocked
When you **rock**, you move gently backwards and forwards or from side to side.

A B C D E F G H I J K L M N O P Q **R** S T U V W X Y Z

rocket
rockets
A **rocket** is a spacecraft that travels very fast. Rockets take astronauts into space.

rode
Rode comes from the word **ride**.
Lucy rides her pony every day. She rode for hours yesterday.

roll
rolls
1 A **roll** is a small, round piece of bread. *Samir had a cheese roll for his lunch.*
2 A **roll** is also a long piece of paper or tape that has been wrapped around itself many times. *A roll of sticky tape.*

roll
rolls rolling rolled
When something **rolls**, it moves by turning over and over. *The ball rolled down the hill.*

roller boot
roller boots
Roller boots are boots with wheels that you wear to go roller-skating.

> **Some words that begin** with an "**r**" sound, such as **wrong** and **wrote**, are spelt "**wr**".

roof
roofs
A **roof** is the top of a building.

room
rooms
1 A **room** is an area inside a building. Rooms usually have four walls and a door.
2 If there is **room** for something, there is enough space for it.

root
roots
A **root** is the part of a plant that grows under the ground. Water travels up the root to the rest of the plant.

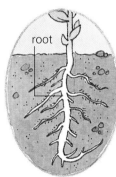
root

rope
ropes
A **rope** is made of lots of threads twisted together. Ropes are often used for pulling things.

rose
roses
A **rose** is a flower with thorns on its stem. Roses often smell nice.

rough
rougher roughest
1 If something is **rough**, it is not smooth. *Rough skin.*
2 Someone who is **rough** is not gentle. *Don't be so rough, you're hurting me!*
3 A **rough** answer is not exactly correct.

---

round
rounder roundest
Something that is **round** has a shape like a circle or a ball.

rounders
Rounders is a game played by two teams with a bat and a ball. The players have to hit the ball and run round four posts.

row
rows
1 A **row** is a line of people or things. *A row of chairs.*
▲ *rhymes with so*
2 A **row** is an argument.
▲ *rhymes with how*

row
rows rowing rowed
When you **row**, you use oars to make a boat move through water.
▲ *rhymes with so*

royal
Someone who is **royal** is part of the family of a king or a queen.

rub
rubs rubbing rubbed
If you **rub** something, you move your hand or a cloth backwards and forwards over it. You often rub things to make them clean.

rubber
Rubber is a strong material that can bend and stretch. Rubber is used to make tyres, balls and boots.

rubbish

1 **Rubbish** is the name for things that you throw away because you do not want them any more.
2 If you say that something is **rubbish**, you think it is very bad.

rude

ruder rudest
Rude people behave badly and are not polite. *It is **rude** to speak with your mouth full of food.*

rug

rugs
A **rug** is a piece of carpet that covers part of a floor.

rugby

Rugby is a game played by two teams with an oval ball. Each team tries to carry the ball across a line or kick it over a bar.

ruin

ruins ruining ruined
If you **ruin** something, you spoil it. *My brother has **ruined** my picture by scribbling on it.*

rule

rules
A **rule** tells you what you must or must not do. *Games have **rules** that you must obey.*

rule

rules ruling ruled
Someone who **rules** a country is in charge of it.

ruler

rulers
1 A **ruler** is a flat piece of plastic, wood or metal with straight sides. You use a ruler to draw straight lines or to measure things.
2 A **ruler** is also someone who is in charge of a country.

run

runs running ran run
1 When you **run**, you move quickly, using your legs. *Kate **ran** after Luke.*

2 When water **runs**, it moves. *The river **runs** into the sea.*
3 When a machine **runs**, it works. *This radio **runs** on batteries.*

rung

Rung comes from the word **ring**. *Tim wants you to ring him. He has **rung** you twice today already.*

runway

runways
A **runway** is a strip of land where planes take off and land.

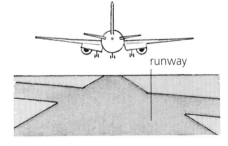

runway

rush

rushes rushing rushed
When you **rush**, you hurry or you do something quickly. *We're late, so we'll have to **rush**.*

sack

sacks
A **sack** is a large bag made from strong cloth or plastic. Sacks are used for carrying things.

sad

sadder saddest
If you are **sad**, you feel unhappy. *Russell was **sad** when his grandparents left.*
■ *opposite* **happy**

> **Some other words for**
> **sad** are **unhappy, depressed, upset, miserable** and **glum**.

saddle

saddles
A **saddle** is a seat for a rider on a horse or a bicycle.

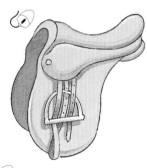

safe

safer safest
1 If you are **safe**, nothing bad can happen to you.
2 If something is **safe**, it cannot hurt you. *Dad mended my bike so that it was **safe** to ride.*

said

Said comes from the word **say**. *Mum asked us to say what we wanted. I **said** I would like some ice cream.*

A B C D E F G H I J K L M N O P Q **R** **S** T U V W X Y Z

sail
sails

A **sail** is a large piece of cloth that is fixed to a boat. When the wind blows into the sail, it makes the boat move.

sail
sails sailing sailed

If you **sail** somewhere, you travel in a boat or a ship.

salad
salads

A **salad** is a mixture of raw vegetables, such as lettuce and tomato.

sale
sales

1 When a shop has a **sale**, it sells things for less than their usual price.
2 If something is for **sale**, people can buy it.

salt
People use **salt** to give food flavour. You can add salt when you cook or you can shake it over your food.

same
Things that are the **same** are just like each other. *Freddie's dogs look the **same**.*

sand
Sand is made of tiny pieces of rock and shell. Some beaches and deserts are covered with sand.

sandal
sandals

A **sandal** is a light shoe with straps that go over your foot. People wear sandals when it is hot.

sandwich
sandwiches

A **sandwich** is made from two pieces of bread with another food between them. *Sam had ham and lettuce sandwiches for lunch.*

sang
Sang comes from the word **sing**. *Aled often sings in concerts. He sang three songs last night.*

sank
Sank comes from the word **sink**. *The ship hit the rocks and began to sink. It sank to the bottom of the sea.*

sari
saris

A **sari** is a long piece of light cloth that you wear wrapped round your body. Indian women and girls often wear saris.

sat
Sat comes from the word **sit**. *Jane could not find anywhere to sit. In the end, she **sat** on the floor.*

satellite
satellites

1 A **satellite** is a machine that travels around the Earth or another planet.
2 A **satellite** is also a natural object that travels around a planet. The Moon is a satellite of the Earth.

sauce
sauces

A **sauce** is a thick liquid that you eat with other food. *Jason covered his ice cream with chocolate sauce.*

saucepan
saucepans

A **saucepan** is a metal pot that is used for cooking. Saucepans have handles and often have lids.

saucer
saucers

A **saucer** is a small dish that you put under a cup.

a b c d e f g h i j k l m n o p q r **s** t u v w x y z

For Internet links, go to
www.usborne-quicklinks.com
103
sausage *to* **sc**rapbook

sausage

sausages

A **sausage** is made from chopped meat that is put inside a special skin.

save

saves saving saved

1 If you **save** someone, you rescue them from danger. *Lisa jumped into the water to save the child.*
2 If you **save** money, you keep it to use later. *Melanie is saving to buy some paints.*

saw

saws

A **saw** is a tool with a handle and a blade. You use a saw to cut wood.

● *See tools on page 128.*

saw

Saw comes from the word **see**.
I see my cousin most weeks. I saw her twice last week.

say

says saying said

If you **say** something, you speak words. *Mark said "Hello" to me.*

scale

scales

1 A **scale** is a set of musical notes that are played or sung in order.
2 A **scale** is also one of the small pieces of skin that cover the body of a fish or a snake.

scales

You use **scales** to find out how much something weighs. *Weigh the plums on the scales.*

scar

scars

A **scar** is a mark on your skin where a wound used to be.

scare

scares scaring scared

If you **scare** someone, you make them feel frightened. *Jessica scared me with her false paw.*

scarf

scarves

A **scarf** is a piece of cloth that you wear round your neck. People wear scarves to keep warm or to look good.

scatter

scatters scattering scattered

When you **scatter** things, you throw them over a large area. *Tommy scattered seed for the birds to eat.*

school

schools

A **school** is a place where children go to learn.

science

When you study **science**, you find out about the Earth, space, people, animals and plants. You do experiments to help you learn about science.

scientist

scientists

A **scientist** is someone who does experiments to find out more about the world.

scissors

You use a pair of **scissors** to cut paper or cloth. Scissors have two handles and two blades.

score

scores

A **score** is the number of points or goals that each side wins in a game. *What was the score of the football match?*

score

scores scoring scored

When you **score** a goal, you make a ball go into a net. *Gavin scored three times in today's match.*

scrap

scraps

A **scrap** is a small piece of something. *A scrap of paper. A scrap of food.*

scrapbook

scrapbooks

A **scrapbook** is a book with plain pages. You stick pictures and photos in a scrapbook.

A B C D E F G H I J K L M N O P Q R **S** T U V W X Y Z

scrape

scrapes scraping scraped

If you **scrape** something, you remove some of its surface by dragging something sharp across it. *Jacob **scraped** the potatoes with a knife. Amanda **scraped** her knee on a rock.*

scratch

scratches scratching scratched

1 If you **scratch** something, you make small cuts in it. *William **scratched** his arm when he fell into the bushes.*

2 If you **scratch** yourself, you rub a part of you that itches.

scream

screams screaming screamed

When you **scream**, you make a loud, high sound. People scream when they are very frightened, hurt or excited.

screen

screens

A **screen** is a flat surface used for showing pictures. Computers and televisions have screens.

screw

screws

A **screw** is a small piece of pointed metal with a flat top. You twist screws into things to hold them together.

scribble

scribbles scribbling scribbled

If you **scribble**, you write or draw quickly and carelessly. *Matthew **scribbled** a note to his mum.*

scrub

scrubs scrubbing scrubbed

If you **scrub** something, you rub it hard. *Rosie **scrubbed** the carpet to get rid of the stains.*

sea

seas

A **sea** is a very large area of salty water.

sea creature

sea creatures

A **sea creature** is an animal that lives in the sea.

sea creatures

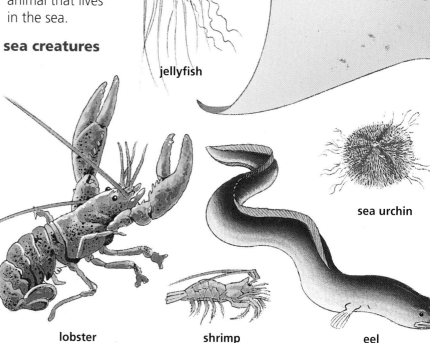

ray

jellyfish

sea urchin

lobster   shrimp   eel

seagull

seagulls

A **seagull** is a large bird that lives near the sea. Seagulls are usually grey and white.

seal

seals

A **seal** is an animal with smooth fur that lives in the sea and on land. Seals eat fish and are very good at swimming.

seal

seals sealing sealed

When you **seal** something, you close it tightly. *Seal the envelope and put it in the post.*

search

searches searching searched

If you **search** for something, you look for it very carefully. *We searched the house for our hamster, but we couldn't find it.*

seaside

The **seaside** is a place by the sea where people go for their holidays. *We love going to the **seaside**, because we can swim and play on the beach.*

For Internet links, go to
www.usborne-quicklinks.com
105

season *to* **se**rve

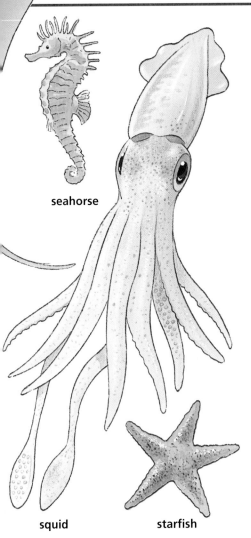

seahorse

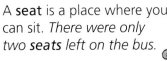

squid   **starfish**

season

seasons

A **season** is a part of the year. The four seasons are spring, summer, autumn and winter.

seat

seats

A **seat** is a place where you can sit. *There were only two seats left on the bus.*

seaweed

Seaweed is the name for plants that grow in sea water. There are many types of seaweed.

secret

secrets

A **secret** is something that not many people know. *We kept Cary's birthday present a secret.*

see

sees seeing saw seen

1 When you **see**, you use your eyes to look at something.
2 When you **see** someone, you meet them. *I saw Suzie in town.*

seed

seeds

A **seed** is a part of a plant. When you put seeds into the ground, new plants grow.

seem

seems seeming seemed

If something **seems** to be a particular way, that is the way it looks or feels. *The journey seemed longer than usual.*

seen

Seen comes from the word **see**. *I want to see Neil. I haven't seen him for weeks.*

selfish

Selfish people think about themselves rather than others.

sell

sells selling sold

Someone who **sells** things gives them to people for money.
■ *opposite* **buy**

send

sends sending sent

If you **send** something, you make it go somewhere. *Josie sent a postcard to her auntie.*

sense

senses

1 Your **senses** help you to find out about the things around you. Your five senses are sight, hearing, touch, taste and smell.
2 If something makes **sense**, you can understand it.

sensible

A **sensible** person thinks carefully and does not do stupid or dangerous things.

sent

Sent comes from the word **send**. *I must send a letter to Marc. He sent me two postcards last month.*

sentence

sentences

A **sentence** is a group of words that make sense. When you write down a sentence, you start with a capital letter and end with a full stop.

separate

If two things are **separate**, they are not joined together. *Jemima divided the flowers into two separate bunches.*

series

A **series** is a group of things that are alike and follow each other. *A series of television programmes.*

serious

1 If something is **serious**, it is important and should be thought about carefully. *We must have a serious talk about your work.*
2 A **serious** person does not laugh and joke very much.

serve

serves serving served

If someone **serves** you in a shop or a restaurant, they help you to buy what you want.

A B C D E F G H I J K L M N O P Q R **S** T U V W X Y Z

set
sets
A **set** is a group of things that belong together. *A chess set.*

set
sets setting set
1 If something **sets**, it becomes firm or solid. *You must wait for the jelly to set.*
2 When you **set** the table, you put knives, forks and spoons on it, ready for a meal.
3 When the Sun **sets**, it goes out of sight in the evening.

several
Several means a small number, usually more than three. *Dan has several pairs of jeans.*

sew
sews sewing sewed sewn
When you **sew**, you join pieces of cloth together, using a needle and thread.

sex
sexes
The **sexes** are the two groups that humans and animals are divided into. One sex is male and the other is female.

shade
Shade is an area that is hidden from sunlight. *Carla sat in the shade because it was so hot.*

shadow
shadows
A **shadow** is a dark shape made by something blocking out the light.

shake
shakes shaking shook shaken
If you **shake** something, you move it up and down or from side to side. *Shake the bottle before you open it.*

shall
Shall means will. *I shall call you tomorrow.*

shallow
shallower shallowest
Something that is **shallow** does not go down very far. *A shallow pool.*
■ *opposite* **deep**

shampoo
Shampoo is a liquid that you use to wash your hair. You rub it into your hair and then rinse it out.

shape
shapes
The **shape** of something is its outline or the way it looks on the outside.

shapes

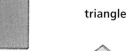

square

rectangle

triangle

pentagon

hexagon

circle

oval

diamond

cylinder

cube

sphere

cone

pyramid

share
shares sharing shared
1 If you **share** something, you let someone else have some of it. *Mary shared the doughnut with her sister.*
2 **Share** also means to use something with other people. *I share the computer with the rest of my family.*

shark
sharks
A **shark** is a very large fish with sharp teeth. Sharks are fierce and can attack people.

sharp
sharper sharpest
1 Something that is **sharp** has a very thin edge or a point that can cut or prick you. *A sharp knife. A sharp pencil.*
2 Something that tastes **sharp** is rather sour. Lemons taste sharp.

shave
shaves
shaving
shaved
When people **shave**, they cut hair from their skin. *Grandpa shaves every day.*

shed
sheds
A **shed** is a small, wooden building. People keep tools and bicycles in sheds.

sheep
sheep
A **sheep** is a farm animal with a woolly coat. Sheep are kept for their wool and their meat.

sheet
sheets
1 A **sheet** is a large piece of cloth that you use to cover a bed.
2 A **sheet** is also a flat piece of paper, glass or plastic.

shelf
shelves
A **shelf** is a flat piece of wood, metal or plastic that is fixed to a wall. You keep things on shelves.

shell
shells
A **shell** is a hard cover around something. Eggs, snails and some sea creatures have shells. *Mandy looked for **shells** on the beach.*

she'll
She'll is a short way of saying **she will**. *Mel is finishing her lunch. **She'll** be here soon.*

shelter
shelters
A **shelter** is a place where you can stay dry and safe.

she's
She's is a short way of saying **she is**. *I'm waiting for Victoria to arrive. **She's** coming at 10 o'clock.*

shine
shines shining shone
If something **shines**, it gives off a bright light. *Hold the torch so that it **shines** on your face.*

ship
ships
A **ship** is a large boat that carries people and things over the sea.

shirt
shirts
A **shirt** is a piece of clothing that people wear on the top part of their bodies. Shirts often have a collar and fasten down the front.

shiver
shivers shivering shivered
When you **shiver**, your body shakes because you are cold or frightened.

shoe
shoes
A **shoe** is something that you wear to cover your foot. Shoes can be made of leather, plastic or cloth.

shone
Shone comes from the word **shine**. *We hoped that the Sun would shine all day, but it only **shone** for a few hours.*

shook
Shook comes from the word **shake**. *We told Andrew to shake the orange juice, but he **shook** it too hard and the lid came off.*

shoot
shoots shooting shot
1 **Shoot** means to use a gun.
2 When you **shoot** in a game such as football, you try to get a goal.

shop
shops
A **shop** is a place where you can buy things.

shore
shores
The **shore** is the land at the edge of a sea, river or lake. *We pulled the boat out of the sea and on to the **shore**.*

short
shorter shortest
1 Something that is **short** is not very long. *A short time. Short hair.*
2 Someone who is **short** is not very tall.

shorts
Shorts are short trousers. People wear shorts when it is hot or when they are playing a sport.

shot
Shot comes from the word **shoot**. *It's Darren's turn to shoot. Gavin has **shot** three times already in this match.*

should
If you **should** do something, you ought to do it. *You **should** brush your teeth every day.*

shoulder
shoulders
Your **shoulder** is the part of your body between your neck and your arm.

shout
shouts shouting shouted
When you **shout**, you talk very loudly. *Kelly **shouted** to Sarah to pass her the ball.*

show
shows
A **show** is a performance that you usually see in a theatre. Shows often have music.

show
shows showing showed shown
1 If you **show** something, you let people see it. *Sophie **showed** everyone her new watch.*
2 If you **show** someone how to do something, you do it and explain what you are doing. *Anna **showed** me how to knit.*

shower
showers
1 A **shower** is a short fall of rain.
2 A **shower** is also a piece of equipment that sends out a spray of water. You wash yourself by standing under a shower.

shown
Shown comes from the word **show**. *Dawn wants to show her photographs to the class. She has already **shown** them to her family.*

shrink
shrinks shrinking shrank shrunk
If something **shrinks**, it gets smaller. *My T-shirt **shrank** when it was washed.*

shut
shuts shutting shut
1 If you **shut** a door, you move it so that it blocks a space in the wall.
2 If you **shut** a box, you put a lid on it.

shut
If something is **shut**, people or things cannot go into it or through it. *The shop is **shut** on Sundays. The door was **shut** and locked.*

shy
shyer shyest
If someone is **shy**, they are quiet and find it hard to talk to people they do not know.

sick

1 If you feel **sick**, you do not feel well.
2 When you are **sick**, you bring up food from your stomach through your mouth.

side
sides
1 A **side** is a surface of an object. *Use both **sides** of the paper. A cube has six **sides**.*
2 A **side** is also an edge. *Milly stayed at the **side** of the pool.*
3 A **side** is also a team. *Which **side** won the match?*

sigh
sighs sighing sighed
When you **sigh**, you breathe out noisily. People usually sigh because they are sad or bored.

sight
sights
A **sight** is something that you see. *A beautiful **sight**.*

sign
signs
1 A **sign** is a shape that means something. *The sign for a pound is £.*
2 A **sign** is also a set of words or pictures that tell you what to do or where to go. *Picnic places are often marked with a **sign**.*

a b c d e f g h i j k l m n o p q r **s** t u v w x y z

sign
signs signing signed
When you **sign** something, you write your name on it.

signal
signals
A **signal** is a message that does not use any words. *The climbers waved their arms as a signal to the rescue helicopter.*

silly
sillier silliest
If you are being **silly**, you are not behaving in a sensible way.

silver
Silver is a shiny, grey metal that is valuable. Some jewellery and coins are made of silver.

similar
If two things are **similar**, they are alike in some ways, but not exactly the same. *Leon and his brother look similar, but Leon has freckles.*

simple
simpler simplest
If something is **simple**, it is very easy to do. *A simple sum.*

since
Since means after. *I haven't seen Mandy since Friday.*

sing
sings singing sang sung
When you **sing**, you use your voice to make music. *Toby loves singing to the radio.*

single
Single means only one. *There was a single rose in the vase.*

sink
sinks
A **sink** is something that you wash things in. Sinks have taps and a plug. *Tom is washing the plates in the sink.*

sink
sinks sinking sank sunk
If something **sinks**, it moves downwards, usually under water. *Tim's shoe is sinking to the bottom of the stream.*

sip
sips sipping sipped
When you **sip** a drink, you drink a small amount at a time. *Richard sipped his hot chocolate.*

sister
sisters
Your **sister** is a girl who has the same mum and dad as you have.

sit
sits sitting sat
When you **sit**, you rest your bottom on something. *We sat on the steps to wait for Rob.*

size
sizes
The **size** of something is how big or small it is. *What size are your feet?*

skate
skates
Skates are special boots that you wear to move smoothly on ice. Skates have a long piece of metal fixed to the bottom of them.

skate
skates skating skated
When you **skate**, you move smoothly on ice, wearing skates.

A B C D E F G H I J K L M N O P Q R **S** T U V W X Y Z

skateboard
skateboards
A **skateboard** is a narrow board with wheels fixed to the bottom of it. You ride a skateboard by standing on it and pushing off with one foot.

skeleton
skeletons
A **skeleton** is all the bones in the body of a person or an animal.

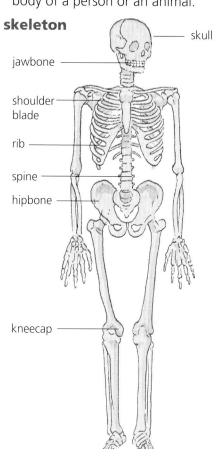

skeleton

- skull
- jawbone
- shoulder blade
- rib
- spine
- hipbone
- kneecap

sketch
sketches sketching sketched
When you **sketch**, you make a quick drawing. *Lucy sketched her brothers while they were eating tea.*

ski
skis
Skis are long, narrow strips of wood, metal or plastic. You fix skis to boots and use them to travel fast over snow.

ski
skis skiing skied
When you **ski**, you travel fast over snow, wearing skis. *Joanna skied down the mountain.*

skid
skids skidding skidded
If you **skid**, you slide on slippery ground. *Noah skidded on the icy pavement.*

skill
skills
If you have a **skill**, you are able to do something well. *Sarah's special skill is drawing.*

skin
skins
1 Your body is covered with **skin**. Babies have very smooth skin.
2 The **skin** of a fruit or a vegetable is its outside layer.

skip
skips skipping skipped
1 When you **skip**, you move by hopping first on one foot and then on the other.
2 When you **skip** with a skipping rope, you keep swinging the rope over your head and jumping over it.

skirt
skirts
A **skirt** is a piece of clothing worn by women and girls. Skirts hang from the waist.

skull
skulls
Your **skull** is the bony part of your head. Your brain is inside your skull.

sky
The **sky** is the space above the ground. You see clouds and stars in the sky.

slam
slams slamming slammed
When you **slam** a door, you shut it with a bang.

slap
slaps slapping slapped
If you **slap** someone, you hit them with the palm of your hand.

sledge
sledges
A **sledge** is a small vehicle that you use to ride over snow.

sleep
sleeps sleeping slept
When you **sleep**, you close your eyes and rest your whole body. Most people sleep at night.

sleet
Sleet is icy rain. It looks like wet snow.

sleeve
sleeves
A **sleeve** is the part of a piece of clothing that covers your arm. *This shirt has long **sleeves**.*

sleigh
sleighs
A **sleigh** is a sledge that is pulled by a horse or a reindeer.
▲ *say slay*

slept
Slept comes from the word **sleep**. *Usually, Anna doesn't sleep well, but she **slept** for hours last night.*

slice
slices
A **slice** is a piece of food that has been cut from a larger piece. *A **slice** of cake.*

slide
slides
A **slide** is something that you play on in playgrounds. You climb up steps and then slide down.

slide
slides sliding slid
When something **slides**, it moves smoothly over something else. *Jo **slid** the book across the table.*

slimy
slimier slimiest
Something that is **slimy** is slippery.

slip
slips slipping slipped
If you **slip**, you slide and fall over. *Duncan **slipped** on the wet floor.*

slipper
slippers
A **slipper** is a soft, comfortable shoe that you wear indoors.

slippery
If something is **slippery**, it is difficult to grip or to walk on.

slope
slopes
A **slope** is ground that goes up or down, like the sides of a hill.

slope
slopes sloping sloped
If something **slopes**, it is higher at one end than the other. *The lawn **slopes** down to the gate.*

slot
slots
A **slot** is a small, narrow space that you put something in. *Put a coin in the slot.*

slow
slower slowest
Something that is **slow** takes a long time to go somewhere or to do something. *A **slow** train.*
■ *opposite* **fast**

smack
smacks smacking smacked
If you **smack** someone, you hit them with the palm of your hand.

small
smaller smallest
Something that is **small** is not as large as other things of the same kind. *A **small** dog.*
■ *opposite* **big**

> **Some other words for** small are **little, minute, tiny** and **titchy.**

smash
smashes smashing smashed
If something **smashes**, it breaks into lots of pieces because it has been dropped or hit. *The cup **smashed** when Robert dropped it.*

smell
smells smelling smelt
1 When you **smell** something, you find out about it by using your nose. *Kate **smelt** the flowers.*
2 If something **smells**, you notice it by using your nose. *That cake **smells** good.*

smile
smiles smiling smiled
When you **smile**, the corners of your mouth turn up. You smile when you are happy or when you think that something is funny.

smoke
Smoke is a gas that is made when something burns. Smoke looks like a grey cloud.

smooth
smoother smoothest
Something that is **smooth** does not have any bumps or lumps in it. *Smooth skin. A smooth sauce.*

snack
snacks
A **snack** is a small meal that you can eat quickly. *We had a snack when we got home from school.*

snail
snails
A **snail** is a small creature with no legs and a soft body. Snails have shells on their backs.

snake
snakes
A **snake** is a long, thin reptile with no legs. Snakes move by sliding their bodies along the ground. Some snakes have poisonous bites.

snap
snaps snapping snapped
When something **snaps**, it breaks with a sudden noise. *The twig snapped when Tim bent it.*

snatch
snatches snatching snatched
If you **snatch** something, you take it quickly and roughly. *Benjamin snatched the letter out of my hands.*

sneeze
sneezes sneezing sneezed
When you **sneeze**, air rushes out of your nose and mouth with a loud noise. You often sneeze when you have a cold.

sniff
sniffs sniffing sniffed
When you **sniff**, you breathe in hard through your nose.

snore
snores snoring snored
If you **snore**, you breathe noisily through your mouth while you are asleep.

snow
snows snowing snowed
When it **snows**, small white pieces of ice fall from the sky.

soak
soaks soaking soaked
When water **soaks** into something, it makes it very wet. *The rain has soaked my trousers.*

soap
soaps
You mix **soap** with water to wash and clean things.

sock
socks
Socks are clothes that you wear on your feet. *A pair of socks.*

sofa
sofas
A **sofa** is a long, comfortable seat for two or more people.

soft
softer softest
1 If something is **soft**, it is not hard or firm. Soft things change shape easily. *A soft pillow.*
■ *opposite* hard

2 Soft also means quiet and gentle. *A soft voice.*

soil
Soil is the ground that plants grow in.

sold
Sold comes from the word **sell**. *Justine decided to sell her books. She had soon sold them all.*

soldier
soldiers
A **soldier** is a member of an army.

solid
1 If something is **solid**, it does not have any air in it. *A solid chocolate egg.*
2 Something that is **solid** does not change shape easily. Solid things are usually hard. Wood and metal are solid.

some
Some means an amount. *We had some soup for lunch.*

somersault
somersaults
When you do a **somersault**, you roll over forwards so that your feet go over your head. You can do somersaults on the ground or in the air.

son
sons
A **son** is someone's male child.

song
songs
A **song** is a piece of music with words that you sing.

soon
sooner soonest
If something will happen **soon**, it will happen in a short time. *It will soon be bedtime.*

sore
sorer sorest
If part of your body is **sore**, it hurts. *A sore knee.*

sorry
1 If you feel **sorry** about something, you feel sad about it. *I am sorry that you are not well.*
2 You say **sorry** when you are upset that you have done something wrong.

sort
sorts
Things of the same **sort** belong to the same group. *What sort of dog do you like best?*

sound
sounds
A **sound** is something that you hear. *Bees make a buzzing sound.*

soup
soups
Soup is a liquid food that you usually eat hot. Soup is made from meat or vegetables and water.

sour
If something is **sour**, it does not taste sweet. Lemons taste sour.

south
South is a direction. If you look at the Sun when it rises, south is on your right.

sow
sows sowing sowed sown
When you **sow** seeds, you put them in soil so that they can grow.

space
spaces
1 A **space** is an empty place or area. *We found a space to park the car.*
2 **Space** is the area outside the Earth. The stars and planets are in space.

spacecraft
spacecraft
A **spacecraft** is a vehicle that travels into space. Spacecraft carry astronauts and their equipment.

spade
spades
A **spade** is a tool that you use to dig. A spade has a long handle and a flat metal end.

speak
speaks speaking spoke spoken
When you **speak**, you use your voice to make words. *Tom speaks loudly.*

special

1 If something is **special**, it is important or better than usual. *A special meal.*
2 Something that is **special** is made to do a particular job. *You need to take special equipment when you go camping.*

speed

The **speed** of something is how fast it moves. *Cheetahs run at an amazing speed.*

spell

spells spelling spelt
When you **spell** a word, you write or say its letters in the right order. *Can you spell my name?*

spend

spends spending spent
1 When you **spend** money, you use it to buy things. *Roberta spent all her pocket money on sweets.*
2 If you **spend** time doing something, you use that time to do it. *I spent half an hour practising the piano.*

spider

spiders
A **spider** is a small creature with eight legs. Spiders make webs to catch insects.

spike

spikes
A **spike** is a sharp point.

spill

spills spilling spilt
If you **spill** a liquid, you let it fall out of its container by accident. *Joel has spilt the milk.*

spin

spins spinning spun
When you **spin** around, you keep turning round quickly. *Melanie spun around as fast as she could.*

spiteful

Someone who is **spiteful** says or does nasty things to upset people.

splash

splashes splashing splashed
When someone **splashes**, they throw water around. *Sarah splashed in the waves.*

split

splits splitting split
If something **splits**, it tears or comes apart. *Nigel's shirt has split down the side.*

spoil

spoils spoiling spoilt
If you **spoil** something, you damage it or wreck it.

spoilt

Spoilt children have too many things and are allowed to do what they like too often.

spoke

Spoke comes from the word **speak**. *Warren usually speaks very quietly, but he spoke loudly to the class.*

sponge

sponges
A **sponge** is a soft material with lots of holes in it. Sponges can soak up water and are used for cleaning.

spoon

spoons
You use a **spoon** to eat and cook with. Spoons have a handle and a rounded end for holding food.

sport

sports
A **sport** is a kind of game that you do to have fun and to exercise. Football and tennis are sports.

spot

spots
1 A **spot** is a round mark or shape. *Laura's dress has yellow spots on it.*
2 A **spot** is also a small lump on your skin.

spot
spots spotting spotted
If you **spot** something, you notice it. *Jack **spotted** some toadstools in the wood.*

spout
spouts
A **spout** is a kind of tube on a kettle or a teapot. You pour liquid out of a spout.

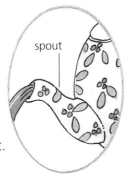
spout

spray
Spray is lots of tiny drops of water or other liquid. *The waves crashed against the rocks and covered us in **spray**.*

spread
spreads spreading spread
1 If you **spread** out something, you lay it or stretch it over a surface. *Hilary **spread** out the map on the table.*
2 If you **spread** something soft, you put a layer of it on something else. *Spread some butter on your bread.*
3 When you **spread** some news, you tell lots of people about it.

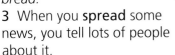

spring
springs
1 **Spring** is one of the four seasons of the year. It comes between winter and summer. In the spring, plants begin to grow and the weather becomes warmer.
2 A **spring** is a piece of wire that is wound into circles. Springs jump back into shape when you press them. Some mattresses have springs inside them.

spun
Spun comes from the word **spin**. *The skater began to spin around. She **spun** seven times.*

squabble
squabbles
A **squabble** is a silly argument.

square
squares
A **square** is a shape with four sides and four corners. The sides of a square are all the same length.
● *See **shapes** on page 106.*

squash
squashes
squashing
squashed
If you **squash** something, you press it and make it flatter. *Nat stood on a tomato and **squashed** it.*

squeal
squeals squealing squealed
When you **squeal**, you make a long, high sound because you are excited or frightened.

squeeze
squeezes squeezing squeezed
When you **squeeze** something, you press its sides together. *Micky **squeezed** the toothpaste tube.*

squirrel
squirrels
A **squirrel** is a small animal with a big, furry tail. Squirrels live in trees and are very good at jumping.

stable
stables
A **stable** is a building where horses are kept.

stack
stacks stacking stacked
If you **stack** things, you put them one on top of another. *Oliver **stacked** his comics on the table.*

stage
stages
A **stage** is an area in a theatre or a hall where plays and concerts are performed.

stain
stains
A **stain** is a mark that is hard to remove.

stairs
Stairs are a set of steps that you use to walk up and down inside a building.

stalk
stalks
A **stalk** is the long, central part of a plant. Leaves, flowers and fruit grow from the stalk. Stalk is another word for stem.

stamp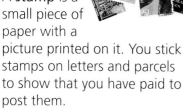
stamps
A **stamp** is a small piece of paper with a picture printed on it. You stick stamps on letters and parcels to show that you have paid to post them.

stamp
stamps stamping stamped
If you **stamp** your foot, you put it down hard on the ground.

stand
stands standing stood
When you **stand**, you are on your feet and upright. *Stand up straight!*

stank
Stank comes from the word **stink**. *My brother's feet stink. After his run, they **stank** even worse than usual.*

star
stars
1 A **star** is a ball of burning gases in space. At night, stars look like tiny points of light in the sky.
2 A **star** is also a shape with points.
3 A **star** is also a famous person, such as an actor or a singer.

stare
stares staring stared
If you **stare** at something, you look at it for a long time with your eyes wide open.

start
starts starting started
When you **start** to do something, you do the first part of it. *Melanie started to tidy her room.*

starve
starves starving starved
If someone **starves**, they become very ill or die because they do not have enough to eat.

station
stations
1 A **station** is a place where trains or buses stop.
2 A **station** is also a building used by the police and firefighters.

statue
statues
A **statue** is a large model of a person or an animal. Statues are made from stone, metal or some other hard material.

stay
stays staying stayed
1 If you **stay** in a place, you do not leave it. *We stayed at home all day.*
2 If you **stay** with someone, you live with them for a short time. *We are staying with my uncle for a week.*

steady
steadier steadiest
If something is **steady**, it does not move about or shake. *You need a steady hand to hold the camera still.*

steal
steals stealing stole stolen
People who **steal** take things that do not belong to them.

steam
Steam is water that has boiled and turned into a cloud of tiny water drops.

steel
Steel is a hard, strong metal that is made from iron.

steep
steeper steepest
Something that is **steep** slopes a lot. *Natalie climbed the steep hill.*

steer
steers steering steered
When you **steer** a bicycle, you move its handlebars to make it change direction.

stem
stems
A **stem** is the long, central part of a plant. Leaves, flowers and fruit grow from the stem. Stem is another word for stalk.

step
steps
1 When you take a **step**, you move your foot forward and then put it down.
2 A **step** is a flat surface that you put your foot on when you climb up or down. *There are three steps outside our front door.*

stick
sticks
A **stick** is a long, thin piece of wood.

stick
sticks sticking stuck

1 If you **stick** two things together, you use glue to join them.

2 If you **stick** a pin or a needle into something, you push it in. *Susannah stuck a needle into her finger by accident.*

sticker
stickers
A **sticker** is a sticky piece of paper with pictures or writing on it. *Fiona has stuck animal stickers all over her bedroom door.*

stiff
stiffer stiffest
Something that is **stiff** is hard to bend. *Stiff cardboard.*

stile
stiles
A **stile** is a kind of step that you use to climb over a wall or a fence. A stile is made of wood or stone.

still
stiller stillest
1 Someone who is **still** is not moving.
2 If something is **still** happening, it has not stopped. *Bridget was still asleep when Lisa arrived.*

sting
stings stinging stung
If an insect **stings** you, it pricks your skin and leaves some poison in your body.

stink
stinks stinking stank stunk
If something **stinks**, it smells horrible. *This cheese stinks!*

stir
stirs stirring stirred
If you **stir** a liquid or a mixture, you move it around with a spoon or a stick. *Paul stirred all the ingredients together in a bowl.*

stitch
stitches
A **stitch** is a loop of thread on a piece of cloth. You use a needle and thread to make stitches.

stole
Stole comes from the word **steal**. *Mum told us never to steal. Dan stole a pencil and she was cross.*

stomach
stomachs
Your **stomach** is the part of your body where your food goes, after you have eaten it.

stone
stones
1 **Stone** is very hard and is found under the ground. Stone is used for building.
2 A **stone** is a small piece of rock that you find on the ground.
3 A **stone** is also the hard seed in the middle of fruits, such as plums or peaches.

stood
Stood comes from the word **stand**. *We had to stand in a queue for the cinema. We stood there for half an hour.*

stool
stools
A **stool** is a seat without a back.

stop
stops stopping stopped
1 If something **stops**, it no longer happens. *It has stopped snowing.*
2 When something **stops**, it no longer moves. *The bus stopped.*

store
stores storing stored
When you **store** things, you put them away until you need them. *James stores his toys in a chest.*

storm
storms
When there is a **storm**, it rains hard and the wind blows very strongly. Sometimes there is also thunder and lightning.

story

stories

A **story** tells you about something that has happened. Stories can be true or made up.

Cassy the Clumsy Crocodile

Cassy couldn't believe her luck when she got a job at Everglades, the biggest shop in town. She tried very hard to be helpful, but the first day she broke twenty cups and saucers and knocked a toy train off its rails.

Worst of all, she dropped a salad on Mr Everglade's head. He was furious, but he gave her one last chance, selling jewellery.

Cassy was left in charge of the jewels, but she wasn't alone. Hiding in the shop were the wicked Greedy Boys. As soon as Cassy's back was turned, they snatched the largest jewel they could find.

Thinking the thieves were customers, Cassy spun round to help them. Her tail caught on a necklace and beads scattered everywhere. The Greedy Boys tripped, but Cassy rushed to help them up. On her way, she knocked over an enormous vase which fell right on top of the thieves!

Mr Everglade was very pleased that Cassy had caught the thieves. He gave her a new job, testing all the sweets and ice creams. At last, Cassy could be really helpful!

straight
straighter straightest
Something that is **straight** does not bend or curve. *Use a ruler to draw a **straight** line.*

strange
stranger strangest
Strange things are unusual, or are different from what you expect. *A **strange** dream.*

stranger
strangers
A **stranger** is someone you do not know.

strap
straps
A **strap** is a strip of leather or other material. Straps are often used to hold things together.

straw
straws
1 **Straw** is the name for dry stalks of plants, such as corn and wheat. Farm animals often sleep on straw.
2 A **straw** is a thin plastic tube that you use to suck drink into your mouth.

strawberry
strawberries
A **strawberry** is a soft, red fruit with tiny, yellow seeds on its skin.

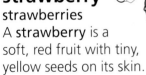

stray
strays
A **stray** is a cat or a dog that is lost.

stream
streams
A **stream** is a small river.

street
streets
A **street** is a road which usually has buildings on both sides.

strength
The **strength** of something is how strong it is.

stretch
stretches
stretching
stretched
1 If you **stretch** something, you make it longer or bigger. *Simon **stretched** the rubber band until it snapped.*
2 When you **stretch**, you push your arms up or out as far as they will go. *Miriam **stretched** up high.*

stretcher
stretchers
A **stretcher** is a narrow bed that is used to carry someone who is hurt or ill.

strict
stricter strictest
A **strict** person makes you behave and do what you are told. *Our teacher is very **strict**.*

strike
strikes striking struck
1 If you **strike** something, you hit it.
2 When you **strike** a match, you light it.
3 When a clock **strikes**, it makes a sound to tell you what time it is. *The clock **strikes** every hour.*
4 When people **strike**, they stop working, to show that they are unhappy about how they are treated or how much they are paid.

string
strings
1 **String** is thin rope. People use string to tie things together.
2 Some musical instruments have **strings**. You pluck the strings to make notes.

strip
strips
A **strip** is a narrow piece of something, like paper or material.

stripe
stripes
A **stripe** is a line of colour. *Harry's shirt has red and white **stripes** on it.*

stroke
strokes
stroking
stroked
When you **stroke** an animal, you move your hand over it gently. *Rachel **stroked** the cat.*

strong
stronger strongest
1 A **strong** person can lift heavy things and has a lot of energy.
2 Something that is **strong** does not break easily. *A **strong** box.*
3 Food with a **strong** taste has a lot of flavour.

struck
Struck comes from the word **strike**. *Our clock strikes every hour. It has just **struck** seven.*

struggle
struggles struggling struggled
If you **struggle**, you try hard to do something difficult. *Bill is **struggling** with his homework.*

A B C D E F G H I J K L M N O P Q R **S** T U V W X Y Z

stuck
Stuck comes from the word **stick**.
Stick your pictures in the album.
I have **stuck** *mine in already.*

student
students
A **student** is someone who goes
to college to learn things.

study
studies studying studied
When you **study** something, you
learn about it.

stuff
stuffs stuffing stuffed
If you **stuff** something into a bag,
you push it in.

stung
Stung comes from the word
sting. *Carol is scared that the bee*
might sting her. She has been
stung *twice before.*

stupid
stupider stupidest
If you are being **stupid**, you do silly
things and are not sensible.

subject
subjects
A **subject** is something that you
learn about at school. Science and
art are subjects.

submarine
submarines
A **submarine** is a ship that can
travel under water.

subtract
subtracts subtracting
subtracted
When you **subtract**, you take one
number away from another. *Ann*
subtracted *seven from twelve.*

12-7=5

successful
Someone who is **successful** has
done well at something.
A **successful** *writer.*

suck
sucks sucking
sucked
When you
suck, you
pull in liquid
through your
mouth. *Alice*
sucked *her juice*
through a straw.

sudden
Something **sudden** happens very
quickly and is not expected. *We*
heard a **sudden** *shout.*

sugar
You put **sugar** in food or
drink to make it taste
sweet. Sugar grains are
brown or white.

suggest
suggests suggesting
suggested
If you **suggest**
something, you give
someone an idea
that might help them.
Sally **suggested** *that we*
should try the other path.

suit
suits
A **suit** is a set of clothes that
are meant to be worn
together. Suits are
made up of a
jacket and trousers or a
jacket and a skirt.

suitable
Something that is **suitable** is
right for a particular job. *Wear*
suitable *clothes for painting.*

suitcase
suitcases
You use a **suitcase** to carry your
clothes when you travel.

sum
sums
A **sum** is a maths question. *I have*
some **sums** *for homework.*

summer
Summer is one of the four seasons
of the year. It comes between
spring and autumn. Summer is the
warmest season of the year.

Sun
The **Sun** is the large, very bright
object that you see in the sky in
the daytime. It gives us heat and
light. The Earth takes a year to go
round the Sun.

sunflower
sunflowers
A **sunflower** is a
very tall flower with
a large centre and
yellow petals.

sung
Sung comes from the
word **sing**. *Maria loves to*
sing. She has **sung** *in*
several concerts.

sunk
Sunk comes from the word
sink. *Some things float and*
others sink. The stone has **sunk**
to the bottom of the bucket.

sunlight
Sunlight is the light that comes
from the Sun. Most plants need
sunlight to grow.

sunny
sunnier sunniest
When it is **sunny**, the Sun is
shining.

sunshine

Sunshine is the light that comes from the Sun. *Go out and play in the sunshine!*

supermarket
supermarkets

A **supermarket** is a large shop that sells food and other things that you need at home.

supper
suppers

Supper is a meal or a snack that you eat in the evening.

support
supports supporting supported

1 If you **support** something, you hold it so that it does not fall. *Support the baby's head when you hold her.*
2 When you **support** people, you help them. *We supported Carly when she got into trouble.*
3 When you **support** a team, you want them to win.

suppose
supposes supposing supposed

1 If you **suppose** something will happen, you expect that it will. *I suppose Justin will be late.*
2 If you are **supposed** to do something, someone expects you to do it. *I'm supposed to make my bed every morning.*

sure
If you are **sure** about something, you know that it is right. *Alistair was sure that he had seen the film before.*

surface
surfaces

A **surface** is the outside or top part of something. *The surface of the table is very scratched.*

surname
surnames

Your **surname** is your last name or your family name.

surprise
surprises

A **surprise** is something that you do not expect. *The party was a surprise.*

surround
surrounds surrounding surrounded

If something **surrounds** you, it is all around you. *The juggler was surrounded by a crowd.*

swallow
swallows swallowing swallowed

When you **swallow** food, it goes down your throat into your stomach.

swam
Swam comes from the word **swim**. *Katherine tries to swim as often as she can. She swam every day last week.*

swan
swans

A **swan** is a large, white bird with a long neck. Swans swim on rivers and lakes.

swap
swaps swapping swapped

When you **swap** with someone, you give them something of yours and they give you something of theirs. *Freddie and Frankie swapped comics.*
▲ *rhymes with top*

sway
sways swaying swayed

If you **sway**, you move from side to side. *Tamsin swayed to the music.*

swear
swears swearing swore sworn

1 If you **swear**, you use rude words.
2 If you **swear** to do something, you promise to do it. *Leo made Rick swear to keep silent.*

sweat
sweats sweating sweated

When you **sweat**, water comes out of tiny holes in your skin. You sweat when you are hot or nervous.

sweater
sweaters

A **sweater** is a knitted piece of clothing that covers the top part of your body. Sweaters are often made from wool.

sweatshirt
sweatshirts

A **sweatshirt** is a piece of clothing that covers the top part of your body. Sweatshirts have long sleeves and usually have no collar.

A B C D E F G H I J K L M N O P Q R S T U V W X Y Z

sweet
sweets

1 A **sweet** is a sweet food that you eat at the end of a meal. *Bethan had chocolate pudding for sweet.*

2 A **sweet** is also a small type of food made from sugar. *James has chosen all his favourite sweets.*

sweet
sweeter sweetest

1 Food that is **sweet** tastes as though it has sugar in it.

2 If something is **sweet**, it is lovely. *A sweet kitten.*

3 If someone is **sweet**, they are kind. *It was sweet of Emily to give me a present.*

swim
swims swimming swam swum

When you **swim**, you move through water using your arms and legs. *Sue swims for the school team.*

swing
swings

A **swing** is a seat that hangs from ropes or chains. You sit on a swing and make it move backwards and forwards. *We have a swing hanging from our apple tree.*

swing
swings swinging swung

If something **swings**, it moves backwards and forwards.

switch
switches

You turn or press a **switch** to make something start or stop. *A light switch.*

swollen
Something that is **swollen** is larger than usual. *Pete has a swollen ankle.*

sword
swords

A **sword** has a handle and a long, sharp blade. In the past, soldiers fought with swords. *A toy sword.*

swore
Swore comes from the word **swear**. *Sam made me swear to keep his secret. I swore not to tell anyone.*

swum
Swum comes from the word **swim**. *I always swim on holiday. I have swum every day so far.*

swung
Swung comes from the word **swing**. *Liza started to swing her bag above her head. She swung it several times.*

syrup
Syrup is a thick, sweet liquid that is made from sugar. *Ann bought some syrup to make flapjacks.*

Tt

table
tables

A **table** is a piece of furniture with legs and a flat top.

tablet
tablets

A **tablet** is a small, dry piece of medicine. People swallow tablets when they are ill to make them well again.

tadpole
tadpoles

A **tadpole** is a small creature that will grow into a frog or a toad. Tadpoles hatch from eggs and live in water.

tail
tails

A **tail** is the part at the end of an animal's body.

take
takes taking took taken

1 **Take** means to move something or carry something. *Take your plate to the kitchen.*

2 **Take** also means to remove something or steal something. *Keith has taken my pen.*

3 **Take** also means to ride in a vehicle. *Dad takes the train to work.*

takeaway
takeaways

A **takeaway** is a meal that you buy and take away to eat somewhere else.

taken
Taken comes from the word **take**.
*Dad takes me to school. He's always **taken** me there.*

tale
tales
A **tale** is a story. *A fairy **tale**.*

talent
talents
If you have a **talent** for something, you do it very well. *Craig has a **talent** for drawing.*

talk
talks talking talked
When you **talk**, you speak to people.

tall
taller tallest
Something that is **tall** is high above the ground. *A **tall** tower.*

tame
tamer tamest
A **tame** animal is not wild and will not hurt people. Tame animals can be kept as pets.
■ *opposite* **wild**

tangerine
tangerines
A **tangerine** is a small, sweet orange that you can peel easily.

tangle
tangles
A **tangle** is a bunch of knots that has been made by accident. *The wool is full of tangles.*

tank
tanks
1 A **tank** is a large container for liquids. *A water **tank**.*
2 A **tank** is also a large, heavy vehicle with a gun. Tanks are used by soldiers.

tap
taps
A **tap** is something that you turn to make water run or stop. Sinks and baths have taps.

tap
taps tapping tapped
If you **tap** something, you hit it gently. *Jonathan **tapped** on the door.*

tape
tapes
1 A **tape** is a long, thin strip of paper, cloth or plastic. *Sticky **tape**.*
2 A **tape** is also a long strip of plastic with sound or pictures recorded on it. Tapes have plastic cases. *A video **tape**.*

tape measure
tape measures
A **tape measure** is a long, thin strip, marked with centimetres or inches. You use a tape measure to measure things.

tar
Tar is a thick, black liquid that goes hard when it is cold. Tar is used to make roads.

target
targets
A **target** is something that people aim at when they are shooting. *Robin aimed his arrow at the centre of the **target**.*

tart
tarts
A **tart** is a pie with no pastry on top. *Jam **tarts**.*

taste
tastes tasting tasted
When you **taste** food or drink, you put it in your mouth to find out what it is like. *Leo **tasted** the soup to see if he liked it.*

tasty
tastier tastiest
Food that is **tasty** has a lovely flavour. *A **tasty** pie.*

taught
Taught comes from the word **teach**. *My dad teaches people to swim. He **taught** me when I was small.*

taxi
taxis
A **taxi** is a car that you pay to ride in. *We took a **taxi** to the station.*

tea
teas
1 Tea is a drink. People make tea by pouring hot water on to the chopped, dried leaves of the tea plant.
2 Tea is a meal that you eat in the afternoon or the early evening.

teabag
teabags

A **teabag** is a small bag of chopped, dried leaves from the tea plant. People pour boiling water on to teabags to make tea.

teach
teaches teaching taught

When people **teach** you something, they help you to understand it, or they show you how to do it. *Monica is **teaching** me how to play the piano.*

teacher
teachers

A **teacher** is someone whose job is to teach other people. Teachers usually work in schools. *Mrs Parsnip is our class **teacher**.*

team
teams

A **team** is a group of people who work together or play a sport together. *Oliver plays in the school football **team**.*

teapot
teapots

A **teapot** is a container that people use to make and pour tea. A teapot has a handle, a lid and a spout.

tear
tears

Tears are drops of water that come from your eyes when you cry. *Tears poured down Harriet's face.*
▲ *rhymes with deer*

tear
tear tearing tore torn

When you **tear** something, you pull one part of it away from the rest. *Doug **tore** his shirt on a nail.*
▲ *rhymes with bare*

tease
teases teasing teased

If you **tease** someone, you say unkind things to them and laugh at them.

teddy bear
teddy bears

A **teddy bear** is a soft, furry toy that looks like a bear. *Fred always sleeps with his teddy bear.*

teenager
teenagers

A **teenager** is someone who is between 13 and 19 years old.

telephone
telephones

A **telephone** is a machine that you use to speak to someone in another place.

telescope
telescopes

A **telescope** makes things that are far away look closer and larger. People use telescopes to look at the stars.

television
televisions

A **television** is a machine that shows pictures and sends out sounds. Televisions receive signals through the air and turn them into pictures and sounds.

tell
tells telling told

1 If you **tell** someone something, you talk to them about it. *Laura **told** me about her holiday.*
2 When someone **tells** you to do something, they say that you must do it. *Mum **told** me to go to bed.*
3 If you can **tell** something, you know it. *I can **tell** that Sam is sad.*

temper

If you are in a **temper**, you feel very cross. *Bill is in a **temper** because his computer won't work.*

temperature
temperatures

The **temperature** of something is how hot or cold it is.

tennis

Tennis is a game played by two or four players with rackets and a ball. The players hit the ball to each other over a net.

tent
tents
A **tent** is a shelter made of strong material and held up by poles and ropes. You sleep in a tent when you go camping.

term
terms
A **term** is one part of the school year. There are usually three terms in a year.

terrible
If something is **terrible**, it is very bad. *A terrible film.*

test
tests
You take a **test** to show how much you know about something. *A maths test.*

test
tests testing tested
When you **test** something, you try it to see if it works properly. *Elsa tested the new recipe.*

thank
thanks thanking thanked
When you **thank** someone, you tell them you are pleased about something they have done. *I thanked Jim for helping me.*

theatre
theatres
A **theatre** is a building where you go to see plays or shows.

their
Their means belonging to them. *Do all the players have their football boots with them?*

them
You use the word **them** to mean more than one person or thing. *I wrote six letters last night. Now I need to post them.*

themselves
Themselves means them and no one else. *The children dressed themselves.*

then
1 **Then** means after. *Eat your tea, then you can go out.*
2 **Then** also means at that time. *I did this painting last year. I wasn't as good then as I am now.*

there
1 **There** means to or at a place. *Have you been there before?*
2 You also use the word **there** to make someone notice something. *There is a cat in the tree.*

there's
There's is a short way of saying there is. *There's lots of food left.*

thermometer
thermometers
You use a **thermometer** to find out how hot or cold something is. *We hung a thermometer in the garden and looked at it every day.*

they
You use the word **they** when you talk about more than one person. *Rosa and Robin are best friends. They go everywhere together.*

they'd
1 They'd is a short way of saying they had. *The boys were late because they'd lost their way.*
2 They'd is also a short way of saying they would. *The girls promised that they'd return.*

they'll
They'll is a short way of saying they will. *The boys have sent a message that they'll be here soon.*

they're
They're is a short way of saying they are. *The girls are excited because they're going on holiday.*

they've
They've is a short way of saying they have. *The Robinsons are away. They've gone on holiday for a week.*

thick
thicker thickest
1 If something is **thick**, it is deep or wide. *A thick book.*
■ **opposite** thin
2 A **thick** liquid does not pour easily. *This syrup is very thick.*

thief
thieves
Thieves take things that do not belong to them.

thigh
thighs
Your **thigh** is the top part of
your leg.

thin
thinner thinnest
1 If something is **thin**, it is
narrow. *A **thin** belt.*
■ *opposite* **thick**
2 **Thin** people are not fat and do
not weigh very much.
■ *opposite* **fat**

thing
things
A **thing** is an object or an action.
*Take your **things** off the table.
There are lots of **things** to do.*

think
thinks thinking thought
1 When you **think**, you use your
mind. *Try to **think** of the answer.*
2 If you **think** something, you
believe it. *Rob **thinks** girls are silly.*

thirsty
thirstier thirstiest
When you are **thirsty**, you want
to drink something.

thorn
thorns
A **thorn** is a
sharp point on
the stalk of a
flower or a
bush.

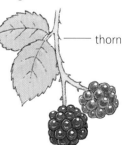

thorn

thought
thoughts
A **thought** is an idea. *Do you
have any **thoughts** about what
we should do?*

thought
Thought comes from the word
think. *We tried to think of things
to do. We **thought** very hard.*

thread
threads
A **thread** is a long, thin length of
cotton or wool. Thread is used for
making cloth or for sewing.

thread
threads
threading
threaded
When you
thread a
needle, you
pass a thread
through the
hole in its end.

threw
Threw comes from the word
throw. *Throw the ball to me. Last
time you **threw** it to Samantha.*

throat
throats
1 Your **throat** is the front part of
your neck.
2 Your **throat** is also the part
inside your body that you use to
swallow food and to breathe.

throne
thrones
A **throne** is a special chair for a
king or a queen.

through
Through means from one side to
another. *We wandered **through**
the woods.*

throw
throws throwing threw thrown
When you **throw** something,
you make it move through the air.
*Judy has **thrown** a stick for Fido.*

thumb
thumbs
Your **thumb** is the shortest of your
five fingers. You have a thumb on
the side of each hand.

thump
thumps thumping thumped
If you **thump** something, you hit it
with your fist.

thunder
Thunder is a loud, low sound that
you hear when there is a storm.

tick
ticks
1 A **tick** is a sign
that shows that
something is correct.
2 A **tick** is also the sound that a
clock or a watch makes.

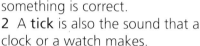

ticket
tickets
A **ticket** is a small piece of paper
or card that shows that you have
paid for something. *A bus **ticket**.*

tickle
tickles tickling tickled
If you **tickle** someone, you keep
touching them with your fingers to
make them laugh.

tidy
tidier tidiest
A **tidy** room is neat, with
everything in its proper place.

tie
ties
A **tie** is a long
strip of material
that you wear
knotted
around your
neck.

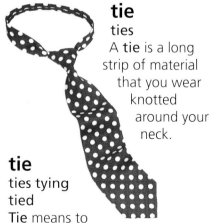

tie
ties tying
tied
Tie means to
hold things together with a string,
a rope or a ribbon. *Jill **tied** a
ribbon round the parcel. Dan **tied**
the boat to the post.*

tiger
tigers
A **tiger** is a large wild cat. Tigers have orange fur with black stripes.

tight
tighter tightest
1 Something that is **tight** is fastened firmly. *A **tight** knot.*
2 Clothes that are **tight** fit closely to your body. ***Tight** trousers.*
■ *opposite* **loose**

tights
Tights cover your bottom, legs and feet. They are made out of stretchy material and fit very closely.

time
1 **Time** is how long something takes to happen. Time is measured in minutes, hours and days.
2 The **time** is a particular moment, shown on a clock or a watch. *What **time** is it now?*

timid
Someone who is **timid** is shy and easily frightened.

tin
tins
1 **Tin** is a silver-coloured metal.
2 A **tin** is a metal can that contains food. *A **tin** of beans.*

tiny
tinier tiniest
Something that is **tiny** is very small. *A **tiny** insect.*

tip
tips
The **tip** of something is the end of it. *The **tip** of a match.*

tip
tips tipping tipped
When you **tip** something, you turn it over. *Henry **tipped** a bucket of water over Harriet's head.*

tiptoe
tiptoes tiptoeing tiptoed
When you **tiptoe**, you walk very quietly without putting your heels down. *Stephen **tiptoed** across the hall.*

tired
When you are **tired**, you want to rest or sleep.

tissue
tissues
A **tissue** is a piece of soft, thin paper that you use to wipe your nose.

title
titles
A **title** is the name of a book, film or television programme.

toad
toads
A **toad** is a small creature like a frog. Toads have rough, dry skin and live on land.

toadstool
toadstools
A **toadstool** is a poisonous plant with a rounded top on a stalk.

toast
Toast is bread which is heated until it turns brown.

toboggan
toboggans
A **toboggan** is a small vehicle that you use to ride over snow.

today
Today is the day that is happening now. *I'm going to a birthday party **today**.*

toddler
toddlers
A **toddler** is a young child who has just begun to walk.

toe
toes
Your **toes** are the parts at the end of your feet. You have five toes on each foot.

toe

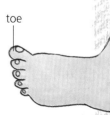

toffee
toffees
A **toffee** is a chewy sweet that is made from butter and sugar.

together

If people do something **together**, they do it with each other. *Sal and Billy played a game together.*

toilet

toilets

A **toilet** is a bowl with a seat. When you go to the toilet, you get rid of waste food and liquid from your body and they are washed away with water.

told

Told comes from the word **tell**. *Can you tell Joanne to come inside? I've already told her twice.*

tomato

tomatoes

A **tomato** is a soft, juicy fruit with a red skin. You use tomatoes to make salads.

tomorrow

Tomorrow is the day after today. *We're going to the beach tomorrow.*

tongue

tongues

Your **tongue** is the long, soft part inside your mouth. You use your tongue to taste, eat and talk.

tongue-twister

tongue-twisters

A **tongue-twister** is a sentence that is very hard to say fast.

> **She sells seashells on the seashore.**

tonight

Tonight is the evening or night of this day. *We're staying in tonight.*

tonsils

Your **tonsils** are the two small, soft parts at the back of your mouth.

too

1 **Too** means also. *Is Ed here too?*
2 **Too** also means more than enough. *The music is too loud.*

took

Took comes from the word **take**. *Mum said we could take a biscuit. Liam took four!*

tool

tools

A **tool** is something that you use to do a job.

tools

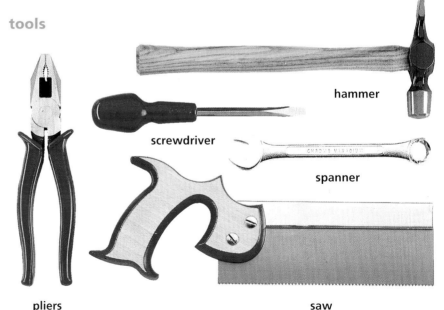

pliers

screwdriver

hammer

spanner

saw

tooth

teeth

1 A **tooth** is one of the hard, white things inside your mouth. You use your teeth to bite and chew food.
2 A **tooth** is also one of a row of thin parts on a comb or a zip.

toothbrush

toothbrushes

A **toothbrush** is a small brush with a long handle. You use a toothbrush to clean your teeth.

toothpaste

Toothpaste is a thick paste that you use to clean your teeth.

top

tops

1 The **top** is the highest point of something. *Carlos climbed to the top of the mountain.*
■ *opposite* **bottom**
2 The **top** of an object is also a kind of cap that fits over its end. *A pen top.*

a b c d e f g h i j k l m n o p q r s **t** u v w x y z

topic
topics
A **topic** is the name for something that you study. Children work on topics at school. *This term, our* **topic** *is weather.*

Weather diary

Tuesday 4th April
Rain all day.
We measured 1 cm of water in our rain collecting bottle

Wednesday 5th April
Sunny and windy.
Our windmill turned round 40 times in one minute.

Hurricanes
Hurricanes are very strong winds. They are like huge spinning wheels of cloud, wind and rain. A hurricane can break up buildings and knock down trees.

Main hurricane

---

tore
Tore comes from the word **tear**. *Patrick must try not to tear his trousers. He* **tore** *his last pair when he went exploring.*

tortoise
tortoises
A **tortoise** is an animal with thick, scaly skin and a shell on its back. Tortoises move very slowly.

toss
tosses tossing tossed
If you **toss** something, you throw it into the air. *Sally* **tossed** *the pancake and caught it in the pan.*

total
totals
The **total** of a sum is its answer or its result. *Four is the* **total** *of two plus two.*

touch
touches touching touched
If you **touch** something, you feel it with part of your body.

tough
tougher toughest
1 Something that is **tough** is hard to break or damage. *You'll need* **tough** *boots for this climb.*
2 Someone who is **tough** is strong and is not afraid of getting hurt.

A B C D E F G H I J K L M N O P Q R S T U V W X Y Z

tow
tows towing towed
When one vehicle **tows** another, it pulls it along. *The truck **towed** our car away.*

towards
Towards means in the direction of something. *Abigail ran **towards** the castle.*

towel
towels
A **towel** is a thick, soft piece of cloth that you use to dry your body.

tower
towers
A **tower** is a tall, narrow building or part of a building.

town
towns
A **town** is a place where many people live and work. Towns have houses, offices, schools and shops.

toy
toys
A **toy** is something that you play with.

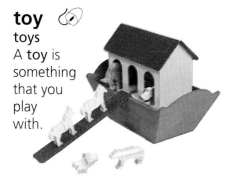

trace
traces tracing traced
When you **trace** a picture, you put a thin piece of paper over it and draw round its outline.

track
tracks
1 A **track** is a path.
2 **Tracks** are marks left by the feet of a person or an animal. *We followed the fox's **tracks** into the wood.*

tractor
tractors
A **tractor** is a strong vehicle with very large back wheels. Tractors are used on farms to pull machinery or heavy loads.

traffic
Traffic is the name for all the vehicles travelling on the roads at the same time. *There's a lot of **traffic** in the centre of town.*

traffic lights
Traffic lights are a set of lights that show traffic when to stop and go. Traffic lights are red, yellow and green.

train
trains
A **train** carries people and things along a railway track.

trainer
trainers
Trainers are comfortable shoes. People often wear trainers to play sport.

tram
trams
A **tram** is a kind of bus that travels on rails in the road.

trampoline
trampolines
A **trampoline** is a large piece of strong material attached to a frame with springs. You jump up and down on a trampoline.

transparent
If something is **transparent**, it is clear and you can see through it. Glass and water are transparent.

transport
Transport is the name for all the kinds of vehicles that take people or things from one place to another. *What kind of **transport** do you use to travel to school?*

trap
traps trapping trapped
If you **trap** something, you catch it.

travel
travels travelling travelled
When you **travel**, you go from one place to another. *We **travel** to school by car.*

tray
trays
A **tray** is a flat piece of wood, metal or plastic that you use to carry food and drink.

tread
treads treading trod trodden
When you **tread**, you put your foot down on something. *Don't tread on the flowers!*

treasure

Treasure is a name for valuable things, such as gold and jewels. *The pirates buried a chest full of treasure.*

treat
treats
A **treat** is a special present or a trip to somewhere nice. *Mum took us to the cinema as a treat.*

treat
treats treating treated
1 The way you **treat** someone is the way you behave towards them. *Sahib treats his little sister very well.*
2 When doctors **treat** people who are ill, they try to make them better.

tree
trees
A **tree** is a very large plant with leaves, branches and a trunk.

triangle
triangles
1 A **triangle** is a shape with three straight sides.
● *See* **shapes** *on page 106.*
2 A **triangle** is also a musical instrument that is made of metal and shaped like a triangle. You play the triangle by hitting it with a metal stick.
● *See* **musical instruments** *on page 75.*

trick
tricks
1 If you do a **trick**, you do something clever and surprising.
2 If you play a **trick** on someone, you make them believe something that is not true.

tricycle
tricycles
A **tricycle** is like a bicycle, but has two wheels at the back and one at the front.

tried
Tried comes from the word **try**. *Lewis will try to move the box. He has tried twice already.*

trip
trips
When you go on a **trip**, you travel to a place and then come back. *We went on a trip to the zoo.*

trip
trips tripping tripped
If you **trip**, you hit your foot on something and fall or nearly fall. *Natasha tripped over the toys on the floor.*

trolley
trolleys
A **trolley** is a large basket on wheels. *A supermarket trolley.*

trophy
trophies
A **trophy** is a prize that you are given for doing something well. *Our team won the swimming trophy.*

trouble
1 **Trouble** is something that is difficult or dangerous. *The farmer had trouble rescuing his sheep.*
2 If you are in **trouble**, you have done something wrong and someone is angry with you.

trousers
trousers
Trousers are clothes that cover your legs.

truck
trucks
1 A **truck** is a large vehicle that carries things from place to place.
2 A **truck** is also part of a train. Trucks are large containers that are pulled by an engine.

true
truer truest
1 If something is **true**, it is correct or right.
■ *opposite* **false**
2 If a story is **true**, it really happened.

trumpet
trumpets
A **trumpet** is a musical instrument made of metal. You play a trumpet by blowing into it.
● *See* **musical instruments** *on page 74.*

trunk
trunks
1 A **trunk** is the thick stem of a tree.
2 An elephant's **trunk** is its long nose. Elephants use their trunks to suck up water and to pick up things.
3 A **trunk** is also a large box that you keep things in.

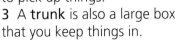

trunk

trust *to* **ty**re

132

For Internet links, go to
www.usborne-quicklinks.com

trust

trusts trusting trusted

If you **trust** someone, you think that they are honest and will keep their promises.

truth

If you tell the **truth**, what you say is true.

try

tries trying tried

1 When you **try** to do something, you do it as well as you can. *Mel tried to climb the wall.*

2 If you **try** something, you test it to see what it is like. *Denise **tried** the rice to see if it was cooked.*

T-shirt

T-shirts

A **T-shirt** is a piece of clothing that you wear on the top part of your body. T-shirts usually have short sleeves and round necks.

tube

tubes

1 A **tube** is a long, hollow piece of metal, plastic or rubber.

2 A **tube** is also a container for soft mixtures, such as toothpaste. You squeeze the tube to get the mixture out.

tug

tugs tugging tugged

If you **tug** at something, you pull it hard.

tune

tunes

A **tune** is a group of musical notes arranged in a special order. Tunes are usually pleasant to listen to.

tunnel

tunnels

A **tunnel** is a long passage under the ground.

turban

turbans

A **turban** is a long piece of cloth that some men and boys wear wrapped round their heads.

turkey

turkeys

1 A **turkey** is a large bird that is kept on a farm.

2 **Turkey** is also a kind of meat that comes from turkeys.

turn

turns

If it is your **turn** to do something, it is your chance to do it. *It's Tim's **turn** to use the computer.*

turn

turns turning turned

1 When you **turn**, you move in a different direction. ***Turn** left at the traffic lights.*

2 If something **turns**, it moves around in a circle.

3 If you **turn** a machine on or off, you make it start or stop.

4 If a thing **turns** into something else, it changes into it. *The ice **turned** into water.*

turtle

turtles

A **turtle** is an animal with thick, scaly skin and a shell on its back. Turtles live on land and in water.

tusk

tusks

An elephant's **tusks** are its two long, pointed teeth on either side of its trunk.

twice

If something happens **twice**, it happens two times.

twig

twigs

A **twig** is a small, thin branch on a tree or a bush.

twin

twins

Twins are two children who have the same mother and were born on the same day. Twins usually look alike.

twist

twists twisting twisted

When you **twist** something, you turn it round.

tying

Tying comes from the word **tie**. *Kim is learning to tie knots. She has been **tying** knots for hours.*

type

types

Things of the same **type** belong to the same group. *Poppies are a **type** of flower.*

type

types typing typed

When you **type**, you write something using a computer.

tyre

tyres

A **tyre** is a circle of strong rubber that fits round a wheel. Tyres are usually full of air.

Uu

ugly
uglier ugliest
Something that is **ugly** is not nice to look at. *An **ugly** building.*
*An **ugly** monster.*

umbrella
umbrellas
You hold an **umbrella** over your head to keep off the rain. An umbrella is made of a piece of cloth or plastic stretched over a frame.

unable
If you are **unable** to do something, you cannot do it. *Leo is **unable** to come tonight.*

uncle
uncles
Your **uncle** is the brother of your mum or your dad. Your aunt's husband is also your uncle.

uncomfortable
If something is **uncomfortable**, it does not feel good.
Uncomfortable shoes.
*An **uncomfortable** chair.*

under
If something is **under** another thing, it is lower than it. *Pickle crawled **under** the gate.*

■ *opposite* **over**

underground
If something is **underground**, it is below the surface of the ground.
*Wild rabbits live **underground**.*

underline
underlines underlining underlined
If you **underline** something, you draw a line under it.

underneath
If one thing is **underneath** another thing, it is in a lower place.
*My toys are **underneath** my bed.*

understand
understands understanding understood
If you **understand** something, you know what it means or how it works.

underwear
Underwear is the name for the clothes that you wear under your other clothes. Vests and pants are kinds of underwear.

undress
undresses undressing undressed
When you **undress**, you take off your clothes.

unemployed
Someone who is **unemployed** does not have a paid job.

unexpected
If something is **unexpected**, you did not know it was going to happen.

unfair
unfairer unfairest
If something is **unfair**, it is not right. *Ivor thinks it is **unfair** that his sister has more pocket money than he has.*

unhappy
unhappier unhappiest
If you are **unhappy**, you are sad or upset.

uniform
uniforms
A **uniform** is a special set of clothes worn by all the members of a group. *A school **uniform**.*

unit
units
A **unit** is a fixed amount of something. Units are used for counting or for measuring things.
*A minute is a **unit** of time.*
*A pound is a **unit** of money.*

universe
The **universe** is everything that is in space. The Earth, Sun, Moon and stars are all parts of the universe.

unkind
unkinder unkindest
An **unkind** person is unpleasant and not helpful.

unlucky
unluckier unluckiest
If you are **unlucky**, bad things happen to you that are not your fault.

unpleasant
If something is **unpleasant**, it is horrible or nasty.
*An **unpleasant** smell.*

untidy
untidier untidiest
If something is **untidy**, it is messy and not neat.

until
Until means up to the time that something happens. *I am looking after Tim's hamster until he comes back from holiday.*

unusual
If something is **unusual**, it is not normal, or is not what you would expect. *Sylvia was wearing an unusual hat. It's unusual for it to be so hot in February.*

up
When something moves **up**, it goes from a lower place to a higher place. *We pushed our bikes up the hill.*
■ *opposite* **down**

upon
Upon means on. *The cat sat upon the step.*

upright
Upright means standing up straight. *The teacher told the dance class to stand upright.*

upset
If you are **upset**, you are unhappy or angry. *Rosie was very upset when her cat died.*

upside down
1 If you turn something **upside down**, you put its top where its bottom should be. *Leon turned the bucket upside down to make a seat.*
2 If you hang **upside down**, your head is below your feet.

urgent
If something is **urgent**, you need to do something about it quickly.

use
uses using used
When you **use** something, you do a job with it. *Jeremy used a pair of scissors to cut the card.*

useful
If something is **useful**, it helps you to do something.

usual
Something that is **usual** is normal and you expect it. *I'll be home at the usual time.*

usually
If something **usually** happens, it nearly always happens.

Vv

vacuum cleaner
vacuum cleaners
A **vacuum cleaner** is a machine that you use to clean carpets. Vacuum cleaners suck up dirt and dust.

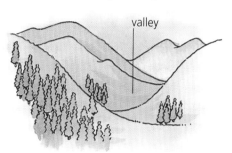

valley
valleys
A **valley** is an area of low ground between hills or mountains. Rivers often run through valleys.

valley

valuable
1 Something that is **valuable** is worth a lot of money. *Mum has a valuable ring.*
2 **Valuable** also means very important. *Valuable information.*

van
vans
A **van** is a vehicle that is used for carrying things.

vanish
vanishes vanishing vanished
If something **vanishes**, it disappears suddenly. *The white rabbit vanished from the magician's hat.*

vase
vases
A **vase** is a kind of jar. You can put flowers in a vase or you can use it as an ornament.

vegetable
vegetables
A **vegetable** is a plant that you can eat. Potatoes, carrots and peas are all vegetables.

vegetarian
vegetarians
A **vegetarian** is someone who does not eat meat or fish.

vehicle
vehicles
A **vehicle** is a machine that carries people or things from one place to another. Bicycles, cars and trains are all vehicles.

velvet
Velvet is a very soft, thick cloth that is used to make clothes and curtains.

verse
verses
A **verse** is a part of a poem or a song. *We sang all five verses of the song.*

very
Very means a lot. *I am very excited about going on holiday.*

vest
vests
A **vest** is a piece of underwear that you wear on the top part of your body.

vet
vets
A **vet** is someone who helps sick animals to get better.

video
videos
1 A **video** is a tape with sound and pictures recorded on it. You watch videos on a television screen. Video is short for video tape.
2 A **video** is also the name for the machine that you use to record and watch video tapes. Video is also short for video recorder.

view
views
1 A **view** is what you can see from a particular place. *I have a view of the beach from my window.*

2 A **view** is what you think about something. *What is your view of this book?*

village
villages
A **village** is a small group of houses and other buildings in the country.

vinegar
Vinegar is a liquid that you use to give food flavour. Vinegar tastes sharp.

violent
If something is **violent**, it is very strong and damages things. *A violent storm.*

violin
violins
A **violin** is a musical instrument with strings. You hold a violin under your chin and move a bow across its strings.
● *See musical instruments on page 74.*

visit
visits visiting visited
If you **visit** someone, you go to see them. *I visited my granny yesterday afternoon.*

visitor
visitors
A **visitor** is someone who comes to your house to see you or to stay with you.

vital
If something is **vital**, it is very important. *Vital information.*

vitamin
vitamins
Vitamins are found in food. You need vitamins to stay healthy.

voice
voices
Your **voice** is the sound that you make when you talk or sing. *Ruth has a high voice.*

A B C D E F G H I J K L M N O P Q R S T U **V** W X Y Z

volcano

volcanoes

A **volcano** is a mountain with a hole in the top. Sometimes hot rock and gas burst out of a volcano.

volume

volumes

1 The **volume** of a sound is how loud it is.

2 The **volume** of an object is how much space it takes up.

3 A **volume** is one of a set of books. *This set of encyclopedias has six volumes.*

volunteer

volunteers

A **volunteer** is someone who offers to do something.

vote

votes voting voted

1 When you **vote** about something, you show whether you agree or disagree with it.

2 When you **vote** for a person, you show that you support them.

vowel

vowels

A **vowel** is one of the letters a, e, i, o or u.

voyage

voyages

A **voyage** is a long journey.

W w

wade

wades wading waded

When you **wade**, you walk through water.

wagon

wagons

A **wagon** was a vehicle used in the past for carrying loads. Wagons had four wheels and were often pulled by horses.

waist

waists

Your **waist** is the narrow, middle part of your body, below your chest.

waistcoat

waistcoats

A **waistcoat** is a short jacket with no sleeves.

wait

waits waiting waited

When you **wait**, you stay in a place until something happens. *Simon **waited** for Sue to arrive at the station.*

waiter

waiters

A **waiter** is a man who serves people with food or drink in a restaurant or a café.

waitress

waitresses

A **waitress** is a woman who serves people with food or drink in a restaurant or a café.

wake

wakes waking woke woken

When you **wake**, you stop sleeping. *Josie **woke** up early.*

walk

walks walking walked

When you **walk**, you move along by putting one foot in front of the other. *Kay always **walks** to school.*

Some other words for walk are **stride, stroll, march** and **hike.**

wall

walls

1 A **wall** is one side of a room or a building.

2 **Walls** are also used to divide areas of land. They are often made of brick or stone.

wallpaper

wallpapers

Wallpaper is paper that people stick to walls. Wallpaper sometimes has patterns on it.

wander
wanders wandering wandered
If you **wander**, you walk around without deciding where to go. *Jonathan **wandered** round the shops.*

want
wants wanting wanted
If you **want** something, you need it or you would like it. *I want some water to wash the car. Helen **wanted** some chocolate.*

war
wars
In a **war**, armies fight each other.

wardrobe
wardrobes
A **wardrobe** is a cupboard that you keep your clothes in. *Ed hung his jacket in the **wardrobe**.*

warm
warmer warmest
Something that is **warm** feels quite hot. *A **warm** day.*

warn
warns warning warned
If you **warn** someone, you tell them about something dangerous or bad that might happen. *Susie **warned** us that the path was very steep.*

was
Was comes from the word **be**. *I will be at the swimming pool. I **was** there yesterday, too.*

wash
washes washing washed
When you **wash** something, you clean it with soap and water. *Mittie and Dan **washed** their dad's car.*

washing machine
washing machines
A **washing machine** is a machine that washes clothes.

wasn't
Wasn't is a short way of saying was not. *Rachel **wasn't** interested in playing the game.*

wasp
wasps
A **wasp** is an insect with black and yellow stripes on its body. Wasps can sting.
See **insects** on page 57.

waste
wastes wasting wasted
If you **waste** something, you use too much of it on something that is not important. *Don't **waste** your money on sweets.*

watch
watches
A **watch** is a small clock that you wear on your wrist.

watch
watches watching watched
If you **watch** something, you look at it to see what happens.

water
Water is the clear liquid in rivers, seas and rain. Water also comes out of taps. People, animals and plants need water to live.

waterfall
waterfalls
A **waterfall** is a place where water from a river falls down over rocks.

wave
waves
A **wave** is the water that rises and falls on the surface of the sea. *The children jumped over the **waves**.*

wave
waves waving waved
When you **wave**, you move your hand from side to side. You wave to say hello or goodbye.

wax
Wax is a soft material that melts when it is heated. Wax is used to make candles and crayons.

wax

way
ways
1 The **way** you do something is how you do it. *Is this the right **way** to spell your name?*
2 The **way** you go somewhere is how you get from one place to another. *Which is the **way** home?*

weak
weaker weakest
1 A **weak** person is not strong and does not have much energy.
2 Something that is **weak** breaks easily. *This chair has **weak** legs.*

weapon
weapons
Soldiers use **weapons** when they fight. Guns and swords are weapons.

wear
wears wearing wore worn
1 When you **wear** clothes, they cover your body. *Max **wore** his green waistcoat.*
2 If something **wears** out, it becomes less useful because it has been used so much. *Jane's shoes are **wearing** out.*

weather
The **weather** is what it is like outside. The weather can be hot or cold, rainy or sunny.

web
webs
A **web** is a very thin net that a spider makes to catch insects.

we'd
1 **We'd** is a short way of saying **we had**. *We'd just reached the forest when it started to rain.*
2 **We'd** is also a short way of saying **we would**. *We'd love to come to your party.*

wedding
weddings
When a man and woman have a **wedding**, they get married.

weed
weeds
A **weed** is a wild plant that grows in a garden or a field.

week
weeks
A **week** is a period of seven days. There are fifty-two weeks in a year.

weekend
weekends
A **weekend** is Saturday and Sunday. *We often go cycling at the **weekend**.*

weigh
weighs weighing weighed
When you **weigh** something, you find out how heavy it is. *Kirsty **weighed** the sugar on the scales.*

weight
weights
Your **weight** is how heavy you are. *Do you know your **weight**?*

welcome
welcomes welcoming welcomed
If you **welcome** someone, you are friendly to them when they arrive. *We rushed to **welcome** our grandparents.*

well
wells
A **well** is a deep hole in the ground. People dig wells to reach water, oil or gas.

well
better best
1 If you are **well**, you are healthy. *Bert is looking very **well**.*
2 If you do something **well**, you are good at it. *Edward plays the violin **well**.*

we'll
We'll is a short way of saying **we will**. *We'll come and see you at the weekend.*

went
Went comes from the word **go**. *Carolyn likes to go to the beach. She **went** there last week with some friends.*

were
Were comes from the word **be**. *The children tried to be quiet. They **were** silent for two minutes.*

we're
We're is a short way of saying **we are**. *We're going on holiday tomorrow.*

weren't
Weren't is a short way of saying **were not**. *We **weren't** allowed to stay up late.*

west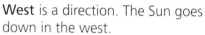
West is a direction. The Sun goes down in the west.

wet
wetter wettest
If something is **wet**, it is full of water or covered with water. *A **wet** towel.*
■ *opposite* **dry**

we've
We've is a short way of saying **we have**. *We've lots of games to choose from.*

whale
whales

A **whale** is a very big animal that lives in the sea. A whale breathes through a hole in the top of its head.

what
You use the word **what** to find out more about something. *What is your name?*

what's
What's is a short way of saying **what is**. *What's the time?*

wheat
Wheat is a plant that is grown on farms. Wheat is used to make flour.

wheel
wheels

A **wheel** is round and can turn in a circle. Cars, bicycles and roller boots have wheels.

wheelbarrow
wheelbarrows

You use a **wheelbarrow** to carry things in the garden. A wheelbarrow has a wheel at the front and handles, so that you can push it along.

wheelchair
wheelchairs

A **wheelchair** is a chair on wheels. People who cannot walk use a wheelchair to get from place to place.

wheeze
wheezes wheezing wheezed

When people **wheeze**, they find it hard to breathe.

when
You use the word **when** to ask about the time that something happened. *When did you last see Mark?*

where
You use the word **where** to ask about a place. *Where are you?*

which
You use the word **which** to ask about one of a number of things. *Which shirt shall I wear?*

while
1 **While** means a period of time. *It's a long while since we first met.*
2 **While** also means in the time that something is happening. *Sam fed my cat while I was away.*

whiskers
Whiskers are the long hairs that grow near the mouth of some animals, such as mice, cats and rabbits. *My pet mouse has very long whiskers.*

whisper
whispers whispering whispered

When you **whisper**, you talk very quietly.

whistle
whistles

A **whistle** is a small tube that makes a high, loud sound when you blow into it.

whistle
whistles whistling whistled

When you **whistle**, you make a sound or a tune by blowing through your lips.

white
White is a colour. Snow is white.

who
You use the word **who** to ask questions about people. *Who won the race?*

who'd
1 **Who'd** is a short way of saying **who had**. *Rosa was the only one who'd seen the film.*
2 **Who'd** is also a short way of saying **who would**. *Who'd like to come?*

whole
Whole means all of something. *Roger has eaten a whole packet of biscuits.*

who'll
Who'll is a short way of saying **who will**. *Who'll come with me?*

A B C D E F G H I J K L M N O P Q R S T U V W X Y Z

why

You use the word **why** to ask about the reason for something. *Why are you upset?*

wicked

Someone who is **wicked** is very bad. *A wicked witch.*

wide

wider widest

1 If something is **wide**, it measures a lot from one side to the other. *A wide table.*

■ *opposite* **narrow**

2 If you measure how **wide** something is, you find out how far it is from one side to the other.

width

widths

The **width** of something is how much it measures from one side to the other.

wife

wives

A man's **wife** is the woman he is married to.

wig

wigs

A **wig** is false hair that fits on someone's head.

wild

wilder wildest

Wild animals and plants are not looked after by people.

wildlife

Wildlife is a name for wild animals, insects and plants.

will

would

If you **will** do something, you are going to do it. *I will tidy up later.*

willing

If you are **willing** to do something, you are happy to do it.

win

wins winning won

If you **win** a race or a game, you come first.

wind

Wind is air that moves quickly. *The wind blew Hattie's hat off.*

▲ *rhymes with tinned*

wind

winds winding wound

1 If you **wind** something round another thing, you put it round it several times. *Rollo wound his scarf round his neck.*

2 When you **wind** up a clock or a toy, you turn its key to make it work.

3 If a road or a river **winds**, it has lots of bends and turns.

▲ *rhymes with kind*

windmill

windmills

A **windmill** is a tall building with large sails. When the wind turns the sails, a machine inside the windmill turns grain into flour.

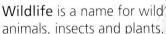

window

windows

A **window** is a space in a wall or a vehicle that lets in light and air. Windows are usually filled with glass.

wing

wings

Wings make things able to fly. Birds, insects and aeroplanes all have wings.

wink

winks winking winked

When you **wink**, you close and open one eye very quickly. You wink to show that something is a joke or a secret.

winner

winners

The **winner** of a race or a game is the person who comes first.

winter

Winter is one of the four seasons of the year. It comes between autumn and spring. In winter, the weather is cold.

wipe

wipes wiping wiped

When you **wipe** something, you rub it with a cloth to make it clean.

wire

wires

A **wire** is a long, thin piece of metal that bends easily. Wires can be used to carry electricity or to fasten things.

a b c d e f g h i j k l m n o p q r s t u v **w** x y z

wise
wiser wisest
Wise people know the right thing to say and do.

wish
wishes wishing wished
If you **wish** that something would happen, you want it to happen very much.

witch
witches
A **witch** is a woman with magic powers who you read about in stories.

with
1 If you do something **with** someone, you both do it together.
2 You also use the word **with** to show that someone has something. *I know a boy **with** green eyes.*
3 The word **with** also shows what you use to do something. *Natasha loves eating chicken **with** her fingers.*

without
If you are **without** something, you do not have it. *Mel came to school **without** his packed lunch.*

wizard
wizards
A **wizard** is a man with magic powers who you read about in stories.

wobble
wobbles wobbling wobbled
If something **wobbles**, it moves gently from side to side. *The jelly **wobbled** on the plate.*

woke
Woke comes from the word wake. *Anne usually wakes up early, but today she **woke** late.*

wolf
wolves
A **wolf** is a wild animal that looks like a large dog. Wolves have thick coats. They live in forests and hunt in groups.

woman
women
A **woman** is an adult, female human being.

won
Won comes from the word win. *Our team hopes to win today. We have **won** our last five games.*

wonder
wonders wondering wondered
1 If you **wonder** what to do, you are not sure what you should do. *Jessie **wondered** which path she should take.*
2 If you **wonder** about something, you think about it because you are curious. *Karen **wondered** what was in the parcel.*

won't
Won't is a short way of saying will not. *Meg **won't** let her brother come into her room.*

wood
woods
1 Wood comes from the trunk and branches of trees. It is used to make things, such as furniture and paper.
2 A **wood** is a place where lots of trees grow close together. Woods are smaller than forests.

wooden
Something that is **wooden** is made from wood. *A **wooden** spoon.*

wool
Wool is the hair that grows on sheep. Wool is made into thread and used for knitting or making cloth.

word
words
A **word** is a group of sounds or letters that means something. You use words when you speak or write.

wore
Wore comes from the word wear. *Kim didn't know what to wear. In the end, she **wore** her jeans.*

work
works working worked
1 When people **work**, they do a job. *My mum **works** in a hospital.*
2 If you **work**, you use your energy to do something. *Zak is **working** hard at maths.*
3 If something **works**, it does what it is meant to do. *Our radio is **working** again.*

world
The **world** is the planet on which we live. The world is also called the Earth.

worm
worms
A **worm** is a small creature with a long, thin body and no legs. Worms live in the ground.

worn
Worn comes from the word wear. *Emily likes to wear big hats. She has **worn** this hat every day this week.*

worry

worries worrying worried
If you **worry**, you keep
thinking about bad things
that might happen.

worse

Worse means less good. *Your
handwriting is **worse** than mine.*

worst

Worst means worse than anything
else. *This is the **worst** film I have
ever seen.*

■ opposite **best**

worth

If something is **worth** an amount
of money, it can be sold for that
amount. *This painting is **worth** a
lot of money.*

would

Would comes from the word **will**.
*I will come to see you this week.
I **would** have come last week, but
I was busy.*

wouldn't

Wouldn't is a short way of saying
would not. *Becky **wouldn't** lend
her brother any money.*

wound

wounds
A **wound** is a cut in your skin.
Wounds are usually quite deep.

▲ *rhymes with spooned*

wound

Wound comes from the word
wind. *Jo started to wind the wool.
She **wound** it round her hand.*

▲ *rhymes with sound*

wrap

wraps wrapping wrapped
When you **wrap** an object, you
cover it with something, such as
paper or cloth. *Ralph **wrapped**
Eric's present in red paper.*

wrapper

wrappers
A **wrapper** is a piece of
paper or plastic
that covers
something.
*A sweet **wrapper**.*

wreck

wrecks wrecking wrecked
If you **wreck** something, you
completely destroy it. *My brother
has **wrecked** my radio, so I can't
listen to it any more.*

wrestle

wrestles wrestling wrestled
When people **wrestle**, they fight
and try to throw each other to
the ground.

wrinkle

wrinkles
A **wrinkle** is a line on someone's
skin. *The old man's face was
covered with **wrinkles**.*

wrist

wrists
Your **wrist** is the joint between
your arm and your hand.

write

writes writing wrote written
1 When you **write**, you use a pen
or pencil to put words or numbers
on paper.
2 When you **write** a story, you
make it up. *Amanda is **writing** a
story about a dragon.*

writing

Writing is anything that has been
written.

written

Written comes from the word
write. *Polly writes to Ali regularly.
She has **written** every week since
she moved house.*

wrong

1 If people do something **wrong**,
they do something bad.
2 Something that is **wrong** is not
correct. *Some of my answers
were **wrong**.*

■ opposite **right**

wrote

Wrote comes from the word
write. *David likes to write poems.
Last week, he **wrote** a poem
about a tiger.*

Xx

x-ray

x-rays
An **x-ray** is a kind
of photograph
that shows the
inside of
someone's body.

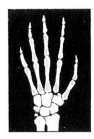

xylophone

xylophones
A **xylophone** is a musical
instrument with a row of wooden
bars. You play a xylophone
by hitting the bars
with small
hammers.

▲ *say
zy-loh-fone*

Yy

yacht
yachts
A **yacht** is a boat with big sails. Most yachts also have engines.
▲ *say yot*
● *See* **boats** *on page 16.*

yawn
yawns yawning yawned

When you **yawn**, you open your mouth wide and breathe in deeply. You yawn because you are tired or bored.

year
years
A **year** is a period of 12 months.

yell
yells yelling yelled
If you **yell**, you shout or scream very loudly. *Felix **yelled** for help.*

yellow
Yellow is a colour. Lemons and butter are yellow.

yesterday
Yesterday was the day before today.

yet
Yet means up to this time. *Maria hasn't rung **yet**.*

yogurt
Yogurt is a thick liquid that is made from milk.

yolk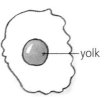
yolks
The **yolk** is the yellow part in the middle of an egg.

yolk

you
You is a word that you use when you speak to someone else. *How are **you** feeling?*

you'd
1 You'd is a short way of saying you had. *You'd already left when I came round.*
2 You'd is also a short way of saying you would. *You'd have enjoyed the film.*

you'll
You'll is a short way of saying you will. *You'll be cold if you don't wear a coat.*

young
younger youngest
Someone who is **young** has lived for only a short time.
■ *opposite* **old**

you're
You're is a short way of saying you are. *You're late again!*

yourself
Yourself means you and nobody else. *Help **yourself** to some food.*

you've
You've is a short way of saying you have. *You've eaten far too much cake!*

yo-yo
yo-yos
A **yo-yo** is a toy that rolls up and down on a string that you loop round your finger.

Zz

zebra
zebras
A **zebra** is an animal with black and white stripes on its body. Zebras look like horses and live in herds.
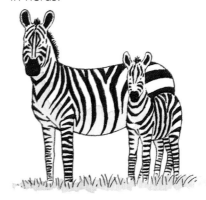

zero
Zero is the number 0. When you take away two from two you get zero.

zigzag
zigzags
A **zigzag** is a line which goes up and down.

zip
zips
Zips are sewn into clothes and bags and are used to fasten them. A zip has two rows of metal or plastic teeth which fit together when you do it up.

zoo
zoos
A **zoo** is a place where wild animals are kept for people to see.

Days of the week

Monday
Tuesday
Wednesday
Thursday
Friday
Saturday
Sunday

Measurements

Length
1 millimetre (mm)
1 centimetre (cm) = 10mm
1 metre (m) = 100cm
1 kilometre (km) = 1,000m

Volume
1 millilitre (ml)
1 centilitre (cl) = 10ml
1 litre (l) = 100cl
1 kilolitre (kl) = 1,000l

Weight
1 milligram (mg)
1 gram (g) = 1,000mg
1 kilogram (kg) = 1,000g
1 tonne (t) = 1,000kg

Months of the year

January
February
March
April
May
June
July
August
September
October
November
December

How many centimetres are there in a metre?

Does March come before May?

Numbers

1 - one	16 - sixteen
2 - two	17 - seventeen
3 - three	18 - eighteen
4 - four	19 - nineteen
5 - five	20 - twenty
6 - six	21 - twenty-one
7 - seven	30 - thirty
8 - eight	40 - forty
9 - nine	50 - fifty
10 - ten	60 - sixty
11 - eleven	70 - seventy
12 - twelve	80 - eighty
13 - thirteen	90 - ninety
14 - fourteen	100 - hundred
15 - fifteen	1000 - thousand

Answers to puzzles

page 3   Alphabetical animals: bear, beaver, caterpillar, chicken, chimpanzee, crab, crocodile.

page 4   Which word?: 1 mouse, 2 fish, 3 shallow, 5 marble, 7 motorbike, 8 musical instruments.
What am I?: kite, rug, fog, bike, book.

page 5   Adding words: One hot day, a thirsty crow called Caspar was searching for something to drink. The stream had dried up and there was no water anywhere. / In the distance, Caspar saw a jug on a table outside a cottage. He flew over to have a look. "Ah, there's water at the bottom," he said. But he could not reach it. Caspar felt more and more thirsty. He tried to push over the jug, but it was so heavy that he could not move it. / Then he had an idea. He flew off to a pile of pebbles and picked one up in his beak. Caspar flew back, dropped a pebble into the jug and then went off to find another. He dropped so many pebbles into the jug that they pushed the water up to the top. At last, he could have a long, cool drink. "All my hard work was worth it in the end," thought clever Caspar.

The publishers are grateful to the following for lending items to be photographed:

Boots (21); Boswells, Oxford (18, 45, 62, 114, 139); British Home Stores (63); Cardew and Company (124); Early Learning Centre (23, 29, 48, 81, 113); Habitat (13, 18, 31, 43, 45, 74, 75, 90, 92, 135); H. Samuel (137); Lewis's (14, 43, 48, 102); Marks and Spencer (112); Mitsui Machinery Sales (UK) (73); New for Knitting, Oxford (62, 141, 143); Next (59, 108, 136); Oddballs Juggling and Kite Company, Oxford (61); Oxford Cheese Company (24); Pennyfarthing Cycle Centre, Oxford (92); Restore, Oxford (130); RPB Warehouse, Oxford (25, 81, 84, 114, 133); Russell Acott, Oxford (36, 74); Tool Club, Oxford (11, 123); Toys Я Us (29); Two Foot Nothing, Oxford (121); Yamaha-Kemble Music (UK) (96); YHA Adventure (27).